METAPHYSICS AND BRITISH EMPIRICISM

METAPHYSICS

AND

BRITISH EMPIRICISM

by

Robert L. Armstrong

UNIVERSITY OF NEBRASKA PRESS · LINCOLN

Chapters 4 and 5 were originally published in somewhat different form as "Cambridge Platonists and Locke on Innate Ideas" and "John Locke's 'Doctrine of Signs': A New Metaphysics" in *Journal of the History of Ideas* (July 1965 and April 1969). Reprinted with the kind permission of *Journal of the History of Ideas*. Chapter 6 was originally published as "Berkeley's Theory of Signification," copyright by the Regents of the University of California. Reprinted from the *Journal of the History of Philosophy*, Vol. VII, No. 2, 163–176, by permission of the Regents.

Publishers on the Plains

UNP

International Standard Book Number 0–8032–0750–6

Library of Congress Catalog Card Number 78–109602

Manufactured in the United States of America

Contents

Introduction

THE PURPOSE of this book is to examine those conceptions of metaphysics prevalent in seventeenth- and eighteenth-century British philosophic thought which are associated with the development of British empiricism. Primarily, I want to determine exactly what the philosophers involved in this line of thought understood by "metaphysics" and similar terms such as "prime philosophy." That the word "metaphysics" is frequently used, often in many different unclarified senses, should be evident to any student of philosophy. The writings of all the major philosophers of this period (Bacon, Hobbes, Locke, Berkeley, and Hume), as well as of many popular literary figures, abound with disparaging statements about metaphysics. Most of the philosophers who attack metaphysics, including all the major ones, exempt some special meaning of the term from their general condemnation. These meanings, too, will be explicated and placed in their proper perspective with regard to the development of the main issues of the period. I want to find out in each case just what these philosophers were against—I doubt that each criticized the same thing. Hobbes, for example, was combating the doctrine of formal and final causes; Berkeley believed that human understanding is capable of solving metaphysical problems but that men make incorrect use of their faculties; and Hume took the view that our faculties are definitely limited in nature and that many problems are insoluble.

An indication of the content of this book perhaps will suggest some of the aims that may be accomplished. Bacon, to begin with, distinguished metaphysics from what he called "philosophia prima." He viewed the latter with some suspicion, regarding it as a "universal primitive and summary philosophy" full of vague conceptions of the beginnings of knowledge. "Metaphysics," however, he defines as the study of formal and final causes and includes it with physics as a part of natural science. Though he admits that in the past improper use has been made of the study of formal causes and that final causes have been mistakenly mixed into physics, Bacon regards the study of formal causes as the "worthiest" kind of knowledge since it is "charged with the least multiplicity." [1] Hobbes, conversely, completely rejects metaphysics as the study of formal and final causes, arguing that they are really just efficient causes and, as such, belong in physics. The notion of cause, traditionally a subject matter for metaphysics, undergoes considerable examination during this period. Hobbes and Locke assume materialistic conceptions of cause, while Berkeley develops a mentalistic theory based on will. Hume, from a skeptical position, finds it unnecessary to postulate an independent external cause of our ideas of sense. Toward the end of the eighteenth century Dugald Stewart defines "metaphysics" in a manner almost the contrary of Bacon's definition. While Bacon considered physics as the study of efficient causes, Stewart placed efficient causes in metaphysics. Because it involved the assumption of necessary connection between

[1] *The Advancement of Learning*, in *The Philosophical Works of Francis Bacon*, ed. John M. Robertson (London: George Routledge & Sons, 1905), 89–91.

ideas, which Hume argued against, Stewart proceeded to reject the notion of efficient cause, assigning it to metaphysics. This was a way of indicating that he considered efficient cause a discredited concept. In the seventeenth and eighteenth centuries one of the most popular conceptions of metaphysics was the notion of a receptacle for discredited kinds of knowledge.

These two meanings of "metaphysics," the study of formal cause and the generic name for discredited kinds of knowledge, should be familiar, but there are several other meanings which are not so well known. Hobbes, for example, reserved a special conception of the role of metaphysics, which he considered legitimate. This is what he calls "philosophia prima," which is concerned with the "right limiting of universal significations," or the definition of basic terms. Similar conceptions of metaphysics occur in the writings of Isaac Watt and Isaac Barrow. Locke's *doctrine of signs* is supposed to be a new science designed as a replacement for traditional metaphysics. It bears some relation to Hobbes's prime philosophy but is more like Berkeley's theory of signification, which also will be examined in some detail.

Yet another conception of metaphysics is that which identifies it with theology. The Cambridge Platonists developed what is sometimes called a "rational" theology, which is based upon a dispositional version of the innate-idea doctrine. They sought to establish the existence of God—a traditional metaphysical ambition—by means of epistemological arguments. I am particularly interested in trying to clarify the transition from this theology to the natural theology of the Newtonians. This evolution is an effect of the development of Newtonian science and, especially, its influence upon religious and philosophical thinking. In the time of the Cambridge Platonists the new science was not quite strong enough to serve as a support or basis for religious beliefs. Rather, the new science was taken to be antithetical to religion by many thinkers of this period, and it was one of the aims of the Platonists to reconcile the new science with cherished religious beliefs. They endeavored to do this by establishing a certain foundation for religious and moral principles in "common notions," which, they maintained, were a necessary condition for all knowledge, including sense experience. The natural theology, conversely, attempted to derive religious and moral principles directly from nature as known through the senses and the experimental methods of natural philosophy. Thus, as the Newtonian science gained in prestige, its exponents sought to associate all legitimate subjects with it. Any subject incompatible with natural philosophy was discredited and relegated to metaphysics.

Some philosophers, respectful of and sympathetic toward natural philosophy, nevertheless thought that there were legitimate inquiries not directly related to the new science. Most significant of these is the problem of the nature of human understanding or the human mind. Philosophers like John Locke, turning away from such traditional metaphysical problems as the nature of reality, were willing to accept the materialistic ontology assumed by natural philosophers and turn to the problem of the nature of human understanding. This inquiry was to become the "true metaphysics," as Hume later called it. That the exploration of this problem was also what his predecessors Locke and Berkeley were trying to do is indicated by the titles of their works which contain such phrases as "Human Understanding" or "Human Nature." So, rather broadly put, a chief purpose of this book is to show how and why "metaphysics" came to mean what we now call "epistemology," or "theory of knowledge," within the historical development of the line of thought known as "British empiricism." A principle factor in this development is the influence of Newtonian science on all areas of thought. Compared to the wealth of discoveries in such fields of natural philosophy as optics and astronomy, ontological speculation became uninteresting. The methods of Newtonian science promised imminent solution to the problems of natural philosophy, and men like Locke hoped to achieve similar success with the problem of the nature of human understanding, a subject they felt had been neglected. It is my suspicion that the history of philosophy is too often studied independently of the rise of Newtonian science. E. A. Burtt's *The Metaphysical Foundations of Modern Physical Science* tries, in general, to show the importance of metaphysical assumptions upon the development of physical science. Another interesting aspect is the other side of this coin, the effect that Newtonian science had upon the course of philosophical thinking, particularly in the areas of ontology and epistemology (metaphysics, that is). There is no big surprise here; we all know that metaphysics suffered a great loss of prestige. But the many new paths that were devised form an interesting, if perhaps minor and little known, chapter in the history of philosophy.

In seeking to understand the shift of metaphysical interest from ontological questions to epistemological ones during the seventeenth and eighteenth centuries I shall be especially interested in exhibiting continuity of thought in the succession of British thinkers of this period. For the major philosophers, Locke, Berkeley, and Hume, this is, of course, well known and well studied, as the currency of the term "British empiricism" indicates. It is my hope that by focusing on the metaphysical aspects of British empiricism I will be able to show further continuity in the thought both of the seventeenth-century philosophers preceding Locke (Bacon, Hobbes, and the Cambridge Platonists) and of philosophers like Reid and Stewart in the generation after Hume. Aside from this basic purpose, I also hope that this special focus on the metaphysical aspects will enable us to see some specific issues in a different light.

Just because we are looking for continuity of thought, I do not think that we are committed to the assumption that it is there: we may look for it and not find it. Also, though we may find continuity between Bacon and Hobbes, for example, regarding the conception of metaphysics, we should be wary of exaggerating its importance. For instance, in a general estimate of the development of the philosophy of Hobbes, the influence of the Continental thinker Gassendi is much more evident than any influence from Francis Bacon. However, our concern is with the different ways these men conceived metaphysics rather than with an explication of the principal sources of their philosophy in general. Hence in starting with a well worked out conception of metaphysics in the thought of Bacon and then looking for traces of it in Hobbes, I do not consider such factors as Continental influences on Hobbes's thought, except to the extent that they may directly affect his conception of metaphysics.

Henry More and Ralph Cudworth, as well as virtually all the minor philosophical writers of the middle quarters of the seventeenth century, were markedly affected by Descartes. He was, however, the only Continental philosopher who influenced to any extent the conceptions of metaphysics developed by the British philosophers after Locke. Even the influence of Malebranche on Bishop Berkeley (his conception of the activity of spirit owes much to Malebranche) is overshadowed by the importance of Berkeley's development of issues raised by Locke.

The historical question, for example, whether Berkeley derived his notion of the activity of spirit from Malebranche, is of secondary importance. The primary philosophical point here is that Locke's account of human understanding was defective because, among other reasons, he overemphasized the passive function of the understanding in perception. Berkeley advances the philosophical analysis of human understanding by stressing the active function of the mind (as in willing). Thus, his analysis does justice to both the passive and the active operations of mind and constitutes an advance on

Locke's position. It is in this sense that I wish to speak of a development in a line of thought—the philosophical development of ideas rather than the exhibition of historical influence. Perhaps some new insight into the main philosophical issues of the period will result from explicating the apparent developmental connections among the positions of a series of thinkers over a two-century span.

Though there is not much doubt from a purely historical point of view that each of the philosophers in this temporal sequence read or was familiar with the work of his predecessor, there are varying degrees of certainty on this point with regard to any two particular men. Nowhere in his major works, to my knowledge, does Hobbes mention Bacon, though we know that as a youth he served as a secretary to Bacon and so must have been familiar with his views. It is pure conjecture, in which I do not wish to indulge, to estimate how familiar Hobbes was with Bacon's views. Hobbes was certainly more familiar with Gassendi's views, for example. What is philosophically to the point is that there is an interesting relationship between Bacon's and Hobbes's views on what metaphysics should be. This relationship is worth exploring, I contend, even if it could be shown that Hobbes was totally unfamiliar with Bacon's position: the philosophical development of the conception of the science of metaphysics is logically independent of the actual historical facts concerning who read whom and who was influenced by whom.

Minor though quite influential philosophical writers of this period, including Bishop Wilkins, Joseph Glanville, Bishop Stillingfleet, and John Norris, who have little to say specifically about the nature of metaphysics in relation to the development of the main lines of philosophical thought in British empiricism are not discussed in this book. Some minor thinkers, like Isaac Barrow, Thomas Sprat, John Keill, and others, are considered because their conceptions of the nature of metaphysics or some aspect of their thought seems interesting or significant within the development of British empiricism. As examples of conceptions of metaphysics during this period which I feel do not have a significant bearing on British empiricism I will now briefly consider those of George Cheyne and Samuel Clarke.

Cheyne's conception of metaphysics is a kind of Platonic realism, but with some rather unusual variations. He tried to unite the principles of Newtonian science and the doctrines of revealed religion in a grand conception of natural religion. He was primarily a theologian and his grasp of Newtonian science was weak. Further, he was wrong in maintaining that religious principles were fundamental to or a necessary part of the methods or corpus of Newtonian science. Though Newton maintained that science and religion were compatible and even that science contributed to natural theology, he was careful to keep the two disciplines apart. Cheyne, in his enthusiasm for Newtonian science and his eagerness to develop a doctrine of natural theology, produced a kind of "weird logomachy resulting from traditional religious and metaphysical doctrines cross-fertilized with conceptions and terms of Newtonian science." [2] Interesting as Cheyne's doctrine is in its own right, his conception of metaphysics is traditional and has no relationship to the major issues of British empiricism.

The same may be said of Clarke, though he is of higher caliber than Cheyne ("Clarke was considered to be the leading metaphysician in Great Britain from 1704, when Locke died, to his own death in 1729"). [3] Clarke defended the theology of his friend Newton against Leibnitz. However, he emphasized the mathematical side of Newtonian science and believed that reason was a more reliable way to knowledge than the senses

[2] Edward W. Strong, "Newton and God," *Journal of the History of Ideas* 13 (1952):166.

[3] *Ibid.*

were. He believed the universe to be mathematical in character, with the elements matter and spirit in its structure, other supposed qualities being modifications of interaction between the two. Clarke was the only one of the prominent followers of Newtonian theology who framed his theology in mathematical terms. Others, like Richard Bentley, William Whiston, and Newton himself, emphasized the empirical side of the Newtonian method and developed the design argument from the premise of the wonder and intricacy of nature. Clarke's conception of metaphysics is traditional, in the rationalist style, and the arguments he develops are out of the line of development of British empiricism.

It is my hope that problems relating to the scope of this study can be handled by adhering to the historical development of British empiricism and sustaining the intention to exhibit continuity of thought. The method of procedure will be to examine the writing of each of this period's major philosophers—Francis Bacon, Thomas Hobbes, Henry More and Ralph Cudworth (the Cambridge Platonists), John Locke, George Berkeley, and David Hume—and to determine their attitudes toward metaphysics, what they understood that science to consist of, and any arguments or positions taken within the field so designated. After making a beginning with the explication of Bacon's conception of metaphysics, we will analyze what each succeeding philosopher had to say about his predecessor's conception. Thus, whatever philosophical continuity there is in this line of thought should exhibit itself. And, I hope, this focus on metaphysics will afford some new insights into the development of British empiricism.

METAPHYSICS AND BRITISH EMPIRICISM

CHAPTER 1

Metaphysics as the Study
of Formal Causes

BACON'S VIEWS ON METAPHYSICS and prime philosophy are given in considerable detail in his *De Augmentis Scientiarum*, which was published in 1623 and is largely a reworking of *The Advancement of Learning*, published in 1605. In the *Novum Organum*, published in 1620, he expounded his new method for the "interpretation of nature" and provided an extensive example in his "investigation of the 'Form of heat.'" If there had been any change in Bacon's conception of metaphysics and prime philosophy as a result of applying his method to a specific problem, and there is reason to expect this, the alteration should be readily apparent in the *De Augmentis*. That any difference between the two expositions is not serious, however, is fairly evident, and the fact of this consistency provides a clue to the solution of some problems regarding the interpretation of Bacon's doctrine of forms and the estimation of Bacon as one of the first precursors of the "mechanical philosophy." [1]

[1] Marie Boas makes this estimate in "The Establishment of the Mechanical Philosophy," *Osiris* 10 (1952): 434–35.

In *The Advancement of Learning*, Bacon begins by dividing knowledge into divinity and philosophy, the latter having three subdivisions. "In philosophy, the contemplations of man do either penetrate into God, or are circumferred to Nature, or are reflected or reverted upon Himself." [2] Before discussing the divisions of knowledge, Bacon marks out "one universal science, by the name of Philosophia Prima, Primative or summary Philosophy" (p. 90). This is necessary, he believes, because the "distributions and partitions of knowledge are not like several lines that meet in one angle, and so touch but in a point; but are like branches of a tree that meet in a stem" (p. 89). He finds in this universal science "a certain rhapsody of Natural Theology, and of diverse parts of Logic: and of that part of Natural Philosophy which concerneth the Principles, and of that other part of Natural Philosophy which concerneth the soul or spirit; all these strangely comixed and confused." It seems to him to be a "depredation of other sciences" rather than "any thing solid or substantive of itself." Nevertheless, he assigns it a certain legitimacy prescribing "that it be a receptacle for all such profitable observations and axioms as fall not within the compass of any of the special parts of philosophy or science, but are more common and of a higher stage" (p. 90). Having given several examples of such axioms—that if equals are added to unequals, the wholes will be unequal; that all things change but nothing is lost; and so on—to show that they are, not mere similitudes between sciences, but "the same footsteps of nature, treading or printing upon several subjects or matters," he finally decides, after doubting whether to do so, to "justly report" the science as "deficient." It is too frequently and conveniently misused to support too wide a variety of particular arguments. That is, the universal science is not so clearly defined and

[2] Bacon, *Works*, ed. Robertson, p. 89. Subsequent quotations are from this edition.

delimited as the special sciences and, hence, it is easy to draw arguments from it to support in sophistical fashion almost any position. Bacon makes these points metaphorically: he sees sometimes that "the profounder sort of wits, in handling some particular argument, will now and then draw a bucket of water out of this well for their present use." But even though this *philosophia prima* is deficient, he indicates that it is capable of future development and, even, that he has fairly high hopes for it. Continuing the metaphor, he remarks, "The springhead thereof seemeth to me not to have been visited" (p. 91).

Returning to his threefold division of philosophy into divine, natural, and human, Bacon first discusses divine philosophy and then proceeds to divide natural philosophy into physics and metaphysics. He issues warning that he uses the word "metaphysic" in "a differing sense from that that is received," but adds that "wheresoever my conception and notion may differ from the ancient, yet I am studious to keep the ancient terms" (p. 93). He then indicates his intention to "recede as little from antiquity" as is consistent with truth and the "proficience of knowledge." As if to illustrate this point, he criticizes Aristotle for taking such a hostile and critical attitude toward his predecessors. It is important to note Bacon's tolerant attitude toward the "ancient philosophy," for it will be a factor to consider when analyzing his usage of such terms as "form."

He considers metaphysics to be a branch of natural science quite distinct from *philosophia prima*, with which it formerly had been confused. Also, natural theology, which "hath been handled confusedly with Metaphysic," is separated and instituted as a special branch of knowledge. It remains to distinguish the two parts of natural science, physics and metaphysics. Claiming the concurrence of antiquity, Bacon decrees that physics "should contemplate that which is inherent in matter and therefore transitory, and Metaphysic that which

3

is abstracted and fixed." Physics is to handle that which
"supposeth in nature only a being and moving," while metaphysics takes care of what "supposeth further in nature a
reason, understanding, and platform" (p. 94). The distinction
at this point seems to correspond in some important aspects
to the Platonic distinction of *The Republic* between the intelligible world of forms or ideas and the world of appearance.
The Platonic forms are fixed and eternal objects of knowledge,
while the world of appearance contains visible objects and
images which are subject to continual change and, hence,
suitable only as objects for belief or opinion. Bacon's distinction differs from Plato's in that he does not ascribe an independent subsistence to the forms but places them in nature as
a platform. This account is closer to Aristotle. Thus, with
respect to the character of the forms themselves and the character of matter, Bacon's account is consistent with both Plato
and Aristotle; but with respect to what I should call the *ontological location* of the forms, Bacon's view is Aristotelian. The
question concerning which is more significant, the character
of the forms or their ontological location, I shall not try to
answer now.

Bacon also utilizes Aristotelian terms in drawing the
distinction between metaphysics and physics. Natural science
as a whole is the "Inquiry of Causes," and these are sub-
divided "according to the received and sound division of
Causes; the one part, which is Physic, enquireth and handleth
the Material and Efficient Causes; and the other, which is
Metaphysic, handleth the Formal and Final Causes." Physics
describes the variable or respective causes, and metaphysics
describes the fixed and constant causes. Bacon cannot report
any of the parts of physics deficient, for they are parts of
knowledge "not deserted by the labour of man"; yet, he finds
himself unable to determine to what degree of "truth and
perfection" they are handled. Regarding metaphysics,

however, he admits that it "may seem to be nugatory and void" because of the prevalent opinion that man is "not competent" to discover the essential forms or true differences. His own opinion is that the discovery of forms is "the worthiest" knowledge to be sought "if it be possible to be found." Significantly, he is optimistic about this possibility and claims that "they are ill discoverers that think there is no land when they can see nothing but sea." Plato is praised for having realized that "forms were the true objects of knowledge," but he is criticized for considering the forms as "absolutely abstracted from matter." Bacon's view is that forms are "confined and determined by matter," and feels that Plato's failure to realize this is the reason his natural philosophy is "infected" with theology.[3]

Though Bacon has warned that he intends to use "metaphysics" in a new way, the novelty of his usage seems to consist in setting up a delimitation of the Aristotelian fourfold classification of causes. The principal element of this classification, the notion of a form or formal cause, he conceives in the traditional manner. He has said that the forms are essential, fixed, and constant; this much is consistent with the Platonic theory. He has added that they are confined and determined by matter, but there is no reason to suppose that he means any more by this than a belief in the Aristotelian theory that forms do not exist apart from individual things. A possible interpretation is that Bacon means by "form" the properties of bodies and that by the phrase "confined and determined by matter" he means that the matter efficiently causes the observed properties of things. This interpretation is in fact given by Marie Boas in "The Establishment of the Mechanical Philosophy," where she cites as evidence a passage in which Bacon claims that error in "this part of Metaphysic" is due to an

[3] *Ibid.*, p. 94.

excessive "departure and too remote a recess from particulars." Miss Boas claims, "As early as 1605, in _The Advancement of Learning_, Bacon proposed as one of the more immediate problems of physics the 'Discovery of forms,' that is, in modern terms, the investigation and explanation of the properties of bodies." [4] It is doubtful whether there are sufficient grounds in _The Advancement of Learning_ for translating Bacon's discovery of forms into "the properties of bodies." For, as mentioned above, Bacon repeatedly refers to the forms as fixed, constant, and essential. This is why he places the discovery of forms in metaphysics and not in physics; Miss Boas misses the significance of Bacon's choice of the term "metaphysics" at this point. The passage that she cites from Bacon begins, "This part of Metaphysics," and in paraphrasing Bacon's remark immediately below the quotation Miss Boas begins, "This part of science." Furthermore, in her first statement quoted above she says that the discovery of forms is "one of the immediate problems of physics." This simply is incorrect, for Bacon carefully distinguishes physics from metaphysics and clearly places the discovery of forms in metaphysics. Perhaps Miss Boas considered this distinction to be of no importance and used "physics" in her statement in a modern sense in order to comprehend Bacon's dual classification of physics and metaphysics. If so, it only emphasizes the mistake of not asking why Bacon chose the term "metaphysics." The answer to this question is that Bacon conceived of forms in a traditional way closely resembling the Aristotelian theory and very far from the mechanistic conception of an atomistic matter causing the observed properties of bodies.

Bacon is well aware of the difficulty of discovering these forms. The forms of substances, he says, "are so perplexed, as they are not to be enquired; no more than it were either

<hr />

[4] Boas, "Mechanical Philosophy," pp. 439–40.

possible or to purpose to seek in gross the forms of those sounds which make words, which "by composition and transposition of letters are infinite." He does think that to inquire into "the form of those sounds of voices which make simple letters" is useful and comprehensible since, once known, it "induceth and manifesteth the forms of all words, which consist and are compounded of them." From this example it is evident that Bacon has the notion that there are a number of simple forms which enter into a great variety of combinations to constitute the complex forms of individual things and substances, such as lions, oaks, or gold. Direct inquiry seeking the form of such objects, he says, is "a vain pursuit," but "to enquire the forms of sense, of voluntary motion, of vegetation, of colours, of gravity and levity, of density, of tenuity, of heat, of cold, and all other natures and qualities, which like an alphabet are not many, and of which the essences (upheld by matter) of all creatures do consist; to enquire I say the *true forms* of these, is that part of Metaphysic which we now define of." [5] There are only a small number of such simple forms, as in an alphabet, and combinations of them make up the essences "of all creatures." This theory is basically Aristotelian.

Bacon is not content to establish metaphysics on an equal footing with physics but stresses the subordinate character of physics. Physics "*only*" (emphasis supplied) deals with the material and efficient causes; it tells us, for example, that the "subtile intermixture of air and water" causes whiteness in snow. This is "well rendered" he says, but adds, "Is this the form of whiteness? No; but it is the Efficient, which is ever but the carrier of the form." [6] It is the form itself and the combination of forms (which is the essence) that are important to Bacon. The form is the object of knowledge, not its "carrier,"

[5] *Works*, p. 95.
[6] *Ibid.*

7

matter, or the various "accidental" efficient causes that may produce it.

There is, however, some novelty in Bacon's view of metaphysics. We find it, not in his conception of the goal of inquiry, but rather in his exposition of the method to be employed in attaining that goal. The discovery of forms, which he recommends as the highest and most useful object of knowledge, was not possible in the past because men had used the wrong methods. Their mistake was to make "too untimely a departure and too remote a recess from particulars." Men tended to abstract their thoughts too quickly and carry them too far from experience. Bacon's originality lies in his attempt to develop a new method, an empirical one which advocates a gradual and cautious assent from particulars, but which adheres to the ideal of simple, general, and certain axioms. Thus, after reporting metaphysics deficient for lacking an adequate method, he nevertheless maintains that it is "most excellent in two respects." The first is that metaphysics fulfills "the duty and virtue of all knowledge," which is "to abridge the infinity of individual experience as much as the conception of truth will permit," by "uniting the notions and conceptions of the sciences." Developing this point, Bacon maintains that "knowledges are as pyramides," and he places history at the base, then physics, and finally metaphysics "next the vertical point." The vertical point itself is the "Summary Law of Nature," but Bacon knows not "whether man's inquiry can attain to it." He concludes "that knowledge is worthiest, which is charged with least multiplicity; which appeareth to be Metaphysic; as that which considereth the Simple Forms of Differences of things, which are few in number, and the degrees and coordinations whereof make all this variety."[7]

The second respect in which metaphysics is "most excellent" is that it "doth enfranchise the power of man unto

[7] *Ibid.*

the greatest liberty and possibility of works and effects." This is, of course, the pragmatic dictum of knowledge as power, for which Bacon is well known. The "disclosures of forms," though highly valued intrinsically, may be "fruitful and important to the state of man," and Bacon often speaks of the benefit of mankind as the chief end of knowledge. For this purpose he considered physics too limited since it revealed only the efficient and material causes of things, but said that "whosoever knoweth any *form* knoweth the utmost possibility of *superinducing that nature upon any variety of matter*" (p. 96). It should be clear now that Bacon's pragmatism is not the sort which would restrict inquiry to merely the knowledge necessary to solve a particular problem. He thought that the goal ought to be to find out the real nature or form of a thing, and he was convinced that such knowledge would give man complete power to reproduce the thing and suit it to human purposes. There is a suggestion here of the old dream of the alchemists: if we want gold we have but to discover its true form, and this knowledge will, by its very character, enable us to superinduce it upon any variety of matter.

When so much is said for Bacon's pragmatism it still remains that he often refers to knowledge as an end in itself, even the highest end man can seek. He speaks of the "dignity and excellence" of knowledge as that which "man's nature doth most aspire" (p. 73), associating it with immortality. This tendency to place intrinsic value on knowledge is quite compatible with his conception of knowledge as being the discovery of forms which are, not merely the properties of things, but the real or essential nature of things. Despite his pragmatism and a suggestion of the old tradition of magic, in the final analysis his basic belief is that knowledge is intrinsically valuable and precedes usefulness.[8]

[8] It is just possible that Bacon's frequent pronouncements that the end of knowledge must be the service of mankind and the improvement

Bacon's express purpose in writing *The Advancement of Learning* was to further the cause of learning and knowledge and defend it against the charges that it is somehow evil and leads to heresy. "I think good to deliver it from the discredits and disgraces which it hath received," he says, for these all come from ignorance, "ignorance severally disguised," appearing in the jealousy of divines, the arrogance of politicians, and the "errors and imperfections of learned men themselves." [9] Bacon was fighting an attitude, prevalent in his time and much more so in preceding periods of history, that knowledge is only important as far as it helps one to lead a good, moral, and religious life. As Bacon says, according to this view "the aspiring to overmuch knowledge was the original temptation and sin, whereupon ensued the fall of man; that knowledge hath in it somewhat of the serpent," and when it enters a man it only serves to "swell" or "puff" him up (p. 44). This is the attitude Bacon sought to counteract by emphasizing the fruits of knowledge as a means to bettering the condition of man. He tried to convince those who held such an attitude that knowledge could serve as a means to increase their comfort and security; by doing so he felt that he could allay their suspicion and win their support for his program to advance the "new learning." Primarily, Bacon's emphasis on the pragmatic character of the inquiry after knowledge was intended as persuasive argument directed at those hostile to the very idea of seeking knowledge of nature. For himself, he regarded the pursuit of knowledge as good in itself and not requiring justification by its fruits.

---

of human life may have been partially motivated by a desire to obtain patronage for "the new knowledge." Thus, it has been suggested that his purpose in writing *The Advancement of Learning* was to obtain the support of James I for carrying out his plans for the furtherance of the new scientific program. James Spedding, Preface, *De Augmentis Scientiarum*, in *Works*, p. 414.

[9] *The Advancement of Learning*, in *Works*, p. 43.

Further evidence for this interpretation may be found in the *Novum Organum*, where Bacon claims that "overhasty and unseasonable eagerness to practice" is often the cause of failure in an experiment. We too often make the mistake of Atalanta, he says, in going aside to pick up the golden apples. Just as God created only light on the first day, we must likewise "from experience of every kind first endeavor to discover true causes and axioms; and seek for experiments of Light, not for experiments of Fruit." [10] He still argues, however, that experiments of light will in the long run produce more fruit, but his use of this argument does not indicate that experiments of light are merely instrumental to the possible fruit they may bear in the future. In practice the ideal Baconian experimentor should devote all his time to experiments of light, the fruit being left to others to gather. Again, in Aphorism 67 he remarks that "when the human mind has once despaired of finding truth, its interest in all things grows fainter." And in Aphorism 99 he states that only when "there shall be received and gathered together into natural history a variety of experiments, which are of no use in themselves, but simply serve to discover causes and axioms" will there be "good ground to hope for the advance of knowledge." It is the light itself, the knowledge of causes and axioms, that is most important to Bacon.

The reason for this discussion of the value of knowledge is not merely that previous studies of Bacon have placed undue emphasis upon his pragmatism but that the conception of the value of knowledge is related to the conception of the nature of knowledge. The nature of knowledge, for Bacon, is the discovery of forms or formal causes which constitute the essence or real nature of things. This view is basically Aristotelian, for Aristotle there is an unequivocal priority of value placed

---

[10] *Novum Organum*, bk. 1, aph. 70, in *Works*, p. 275.

upon knowledge itself as opposed to any "fruits" of knowledge. To Aristotle the end of theoretical knowledge is truth and, though practical knowledge is recognized, there is no suggestion that the former is supposed to be subordinated to the latter. If there is a connection between the conception of the nature of knowledge and the value of knowledge, then, since Aristotle and Bacon held similar conceptions of the nature of knowledge, it would be expected that they would hold similar conceptions concerning the value of knowledge.

Bacon's conception of metaphysics as the study of formal causes constitutes at once a statement about the nature of knowledge and the goal of natural philosophy. That he considered such a statement to be of primary importance is beyond doubt. Failure to realize the importance of his conception of metaphysics, especially its relation to his inductive method, is the cause of much misunderstanding of Bacon and his place in the development of seventeenth-century science and philosophy. Before this point can be made clear there are some further details relating to his conception of metaphysics in *The Advancement of Learning* that must be explicated.

The study of forms is only the first part of metaphysics; there is also a second part, "the inquiry of *final* causes." Bacon is critical of this kind of inquiry, not because final causes are not true and "worthy to be inquired," but because they have been "misplaced." And, "this misplacing hath caused a deficience, or at least a great inproficience in the sciences themselves." Further, "the handling of final causes mixed with the rest of physical inquiries, hath intercepted the severe and diligent inquiry of all real and physical causes, and given men the occasion to stay upon these satisfactory and specious causes, to the great arrest and prejudice of further discovery." This has been done "not only by Plato, who ever anchoreth upon that shore, but by Aristotle, Galen, and others." After giving some examples of explanations in terms of final causes, he remarks that these are "well enquired and collected in Metaphysic; but in Physic they are impertinent." It is at this point that Bacon expresses his preference for the natural philosophy of Democritus because he did not suppose "a mind or reason in the frame of things." It is important to notice, however, that Bacon's preference for Democritus over Aristotle and Plato is not unqualified. He says that the natural philosophy of Democritus "seemeth to me . . . *in particularities of physical causes* more real and better enquired than those of Aristotle and Plato." [11] Bacon has already made a considerable point of distinguishing the study of the different kinds of causes, assigning them to different sciences, and therefore we must take him quite seriously when he qualifies his remarks with a reference to some one kind of cause. By "physical causes" here he means material and efficient causes, which are the subject matter of physics. In effect, then, he is saying that the physics of Democritus is better than the physics of Plato and Aristotle. But his ground for this decision is not, as one might suppose, that the theory of forms common to Plato and Aristotle is defective but rather that these two philosophers have "intermingled final causes, the one as a part of theology, and the other as a part of logic" (*ibid.*).

Two points should be considered regarding Bacon's position on final causes. In the first place one might emphasize both his strong statements about the detrimental effect of considering such causes in physics and about his preference for Democritus, and think that Bacon is rejecting completely the Platonic and Aristotelian philosophy of forms. This is a mistake because the forms constitute his conception of the nature of knowledge. They are the ultimate object of inquiry, to which physical causes, efficient and material, are clearly subordinated. Bacon's preference for Democritus over Plato and Aristotle, as he says himself, is limited to the subject of physical causes

[11] *The Advancement of Learning*, in *Works*, p. 96. Emphasis supplied.

and is quite consistent with his earlier remarks to the effect that forms are the true object of knowledge. On this issue he considers Plato and Aristotle preferable to Democritus. The second point regarding final causes is that Bacon does not intend to discredit them entirely. One might suppose this if one ignored Bacon's remarks about metaphysics and assumed that he considered physics to be the all-important science. According to this view, to exclude final causes from physics is tantamount to entirely discrediting them. However, since Bacon does not ascribe primary importance to physics, though freeing it from final causes, he maintains that inquiry into final causes is a legitimate undertaking of metaphysics. Provided that the final cause is not mixed with physical causes, "men are extremely deceived if they think there is an enmity or repugnancy at all between them." Again, regarding an example of two statements, one ascribing an efficient cause and the other a final cause, he says that "both causes [may be] true and compatible, the one declaring an intention, the other a consequence only" (*ibid.*).

Though Bacon claims to have concluded his discussion of metaphysics at this point, he remarks that there is yet another part of natural philosophy, mathematics, which "holdeth rank with Physic special and Metaphysic." He adds, however, that he thinks it "more agreeable to the nature of things and to the light of order to place it as a branch of Metaphysic." His reason is that the subject of mathematics is "quantity determined or proportionable" and this "appeareth to be one of the Essential Forms of things." He claims the authority of both Democritus and Pythagoras on this point and adds that, of all forms, it is "the most abstracted and separable from matter, and therefore most proper to Metaphysic." Because this is so, mathematics "hath been better laboured and enquired" since, he says, it is the "nature of the mind of man (to the extreme prejudice of knowledge) to delight in the spacious liberty of generalities."[12] Mathematics, being most free among the sciences of particularity and matter, best satisfies this appetite. In the *Novum Organum*, Bacon clearly maintains that the greatest error that has been committed by his predecessors, is that they were too anxious to leave particulars and immediately jump to general principles. Thus, the chief point of his method is the recommendation to exercise caution in making this jump; we should seek axioms and principles not so far removed from the particulars. It is easy to see why he should be somewhat suspicious of mathematics, a discipline remote from the examination of particulars. If Bacon is wary and yet says that mathematics is most properly a part of metaphysics, then it would seem that metaphysics too is somewhat under suspicion. This suggestion is at variance with Bacon's earlier praise of metaphysics and with the place he assigns to it close to the apex of knowledge attainable through theoretical inquiry.

This suspected difficulty is not so serious as it may appear. Bacon's attitude toward mathematics is similar to his attitude toward the Platonic theory of forms. He praises Plato for realizing that forms are the true object of inquiry but criticizes him for completely detaching, or, as he says, "abstracting," them from matter. Since mathematics is a subject more abstracted from matter than any other, it is exposed both to suspicion for being too remote from particulars and to the error of overhasty generalization. Metaphysics, and mathematics as a part of it, is a legitimate science since a method is employed which permits cautious and gradual assent from particulars to the general axioms. Bacon thought he had devised just such a method, and we must now turn to it.

The best statement of Bacon's method and his application of it to the " Nature of Heat " are in the second book of the *Novum Organum*, published fifteen years after *The Advancement*

[12] *Ibid.*, p. 97.

of Learning. Bacon begins by reaffirming the view that "knowledge is knowledge by causes," causes being divided into four kinds. The final cause, he remarks, "rather corrupts" the sciences, the discovery of the formal "is despaired of," and the efficient and material "are but slight and superficial." He has said these things before, but he now has something new to say about the nature of the formal cause: "For though in nature nothing really exists beside individual bodies, performing pure individual acts according to a fixed law, yet in philosophy this very law, and investigation, discovery and explanation of it, is the foundation as well of knowledge as of operation. And it is this law, with its clauses, that I mean when I speak of *Forms;* a name which I the rather adopt because it has grown into use and become familiar."[13] It is on the basis of this passage and some others like it that Bacon is rated along with Galileo as a precursor of the mechanical philosophy of the seventeenth century. Mechanical philosophy as it appears later in that century almost always involves three elements: (1) some kind of atomic or corpuscular theory of matter, (2) a conception of mathematical laws which govern physical events, and (3) the theory that the motion of particles efficiently causes the observed properties of things. All these elements are present in the philosophies of Galileo, Descartes, Hobbes, and Newton. The passage from Bacon appears to contain two elements—the conception of mathematical law and a theory of material atomism—but there is no indication in this passage or in later ones that Bacon has any conception of material atoms efficiently causing ideas of sense. Furthermore, his conception of mathematical law is quite unlike Galileo's, Descartes's and Newton's: Bacon appears to know very little mathematics. If Bacon had had any clear idea of the theory of material particles efficiently causing ideas in the mind, he would have conceived the goal of natural philosophy

[13] *Novum Organum*, bk. 2, aph. 2, in *Works*, pp. 302–3.

in terms of efficient and material causes. Instead of this he chose formal cause as the goal of inquiry and even after a detailed application of his experimental method he still thought of forms in the traditional Aristotelian way as the end of knowledge. The choice of form or formal cause for this purpose was not simply a matter of terminology as he suggests but indicates an entirely different conception of the nature of knowledge from that of the mechanistic natural philosophers of the seventeenth century.

As to method Bacon says in Aphorism 19 of Book 1 (p. 261), that there are "and can only be two ways of searching into and discovering truth." The first one "flies from the senses and particulars to the most general axioms, and from these principles, the truth of which it takes for settled and immoveable, proceeds to judgement and to the discovery of middle axioms." This is the method currently in fashion, he remarks, and we are familiar with his criticism of it: it departs too soon and goes too far from the particulars, and this excessive eagerness to get to the most general axioms is the cause of error. The second method "derives axioms from the senses and particulars, rising by a gradual and unbroken ascent, so that it arrives at the most general axioms last of all." "This is the true way," but it is as yet "untried," he states. The understanding "left to itself" prefers the first method, "for the mind longs to spring up to positions of higher generality, that it may find rest there" (bk. 1, aph. 20, p. 261). Thus, it "wearies of experiment," and this "evil" is increased by logic and, presumably, mathematics. But, though the difference between the two methods is "infinite," it is most important to be clear about just what that difference is supposed to be. One might think that Bacon objects to these "highest axioms" and intends to disparage them entirely. This is not the case, for he says that "both ways set out from the senses and particulars, *and rest in the highest generalities*" (aph. 22, p. 261;

emphasis supplied). Bacon is not against these highest axioms as such, for they are equally the goal of his method and of the "traditional" method he criticizes. What is important to Bacon is that procedure should be gradual, going step by step from particulars through a series of "middle axioms" to the highest axioms. It is, in his view, only then that there is a chance of being right in the conception of the highest axioms. There would then be an unbroken chain of generalizations linking the particulars to the highest axioms. Only when the axioms were obtained in this way would there be an assurance of being able to reverse the process and derive new experiments from the axioms. Bacon was as much interested in these highest axioms as any seventeenth-century rationalist or medieval scholastic. They have the traditional value, which Bacon approves, of disclosing the "unity of nature" as well as the "new" value of "discovering further experiments." [14]

It appears, then, that Bacon, at least, saw no incompatibility between this method and its supposed goal. However, in the attempt to develop a new experimental method for the purpose of achieving what was essentially the same ideal of knowledge held by Aristotle, one might expect some incompatibility. There are numerous passages in Bacon where he warns us that his conception of form is different from the "traditional" or "received" meaning, but these warnings are, for the most part, empty. We have plenty of valid reasons for expecting a new goal to go with a new method, and it has been

[14] It should be understood that "axioms" are the expressions in language of the forms, either formal or final. A form expressed in language is an axiom. A form referred to as it exists in a physical thing is called an "essence" or "nature." When Bacon speaks of the discovery of "the highest axioms" as the goal of inquiry, he refers to a projected body of knowledge organized logically. When he speaks of the discovery of forms as the task of metaphysics, he refers to what he takes to be common to the nature or essence of things and to the knowing mind. See further discussion below.

almost common practice for scholars to assume or read this new goal into Bacon.

One scholar, for example, after remarking that the discovery of the "true and lawful method" was the only "glory" that Bacon claimed for himself, then adds, "But his conception of the method of knowledge is determined by his conception of the nature, or rather the true object and goal, of knowledge." This is just what is not true and, considering Bacon's conception of the knowledge of nature, the same writer states that it "can obviously, not relate to the highest generalities." [15] Furthermore, "it is not such knowledge as the metaphysical philosopher seeks, when he inquires concerning the ultimate essence and ground of physical existence. It is the knowledge of the proximate causes and observable laws of phenomena" (pp. 132–33). If this interpretation were correct, we should expect to find Bacon referring to the goal and method of knowledge in terms of efficient and material causes. However, immediately after speaking of forms as the "fixed law" according to which bodies act, Bacon remarks:

> Now if a man's knowledge be confined to the efficient and material causes (which are unstable causes, and merely vehicles, or causes which convey the form in certain cases) he may arrive at new discoveries in reference to substances in some degree similar to one another, and selected beforehand; *but he does not touch the deeper boundaries of things.* But whosoever is acquainted with Forms, embraces the unity of nature in substances the most unlike; and is able therefore to detect and bring to light things never yet done, and such as neither the vicissitudes of nature, nor industry in experimenting nor accident itself, would ever have brought into act, and which would never have occurred to the thought of man. From the discovery of Forms therefore results truth in speculation and freedom in operation.[16]

[15] George S. Morris, *British Thought and Thinkers* (Chicago: S. C. Griggs & Co., 1880), p. 131.

[16] *Novum Organum*, bk. 2, aph. 3, in *Works*, p. 303. Emphasis supplied.

Does this sound like a man concerned merely with the "proximate causes and observable laws of phenomena"? Bacon is not satisfied with proximate or efficient causes, nor is he satisfied with merely observable laws; he is concerned with the "deeper boundaries of things," and this is why he designates the object of knowledge as the forms of things which are supposed to be, in his own words, "inherent in the nature of a thing."

Not only are the forms inherent in things and more than properties and observable laws but also they are supposed to be related to one another in something like the Aristotelian classificatory system of genus and species. Bacon remarks that "the true Form is such that it deduces the given nature from some source of being which is inherent in more natures, and which is better known in the natural order of things than the Form itself." Presumably, the "source of being which is inherent in more natures" is some more general form which exhibits itself in a class of other and possibly diverse forms (much as the genus is related to the species subsumed under it or as the universal subsumes the particular). Thus, Bacon advances as a "true and perfect axiom of knowledge" the precept that "another nature be discovered which is convertible with the given nature, and yet is a limitation of a more general nature, *as of a true and real genus.*"[17] It now appears, then, that when Bacon speaks of the forms as fixed laws governing the acts of individual bodies his idea of law is different from the notion of mathematical law that was characteristic of Galileo and the seventeenth-century mechanistic philosophers. Bacon's notion of law is something like the Aristotelian hierarchical classification involving inherence and subsumption.

It is possible to emphasize Bacon's many references to "combinations of forms" which constitute physical objects

[17] *Ibid.*, aph. 4, p. 303. Emphasis supplied.

and interpret forms as something like the elements of modern physical theory. Thus, there are simple forms or elements which combine to make composite things according to laws. Bacon, then, can be called a precursor of modern science. Against this interpretation it should be noticed that Bacon speaks of forms as ordered in a kind of Aristotelian hierarchical classification quite as often as he speaks of them as combining to form composite physical things. This fact alone is good evidence that he thought in terms of the traditional formistic theory, with its parallel realms of being and knowledge. It is perfectly correct that Bacon regarded the nature of physical things as a combination of simple forms, but it is also the case that when he wanted to speak of the form itself he found it necessary to classify it in the traditional Aristotelian manner. He makes it clear that knowledge is the goal to be achieved, and he understood knowledge as consisting of an ordered hierarchy of axioms progressing from the most particular to the highest or most general. The interpretation of Bacon as a precursor of a theory of elements combining according to laws requires that his axioms be something like mathematical laws, which they are not for his experimental method makes no use of that subject. His axioms are either particular or general or lower or higher and could hardly be anything like the laws that are supposed to govern the combination of elements in modern physical theory.

At this point the discussion becomes more complex because Bacon explicitly recognizes a distinction that has been implicit all along. In previous statements about forms there has often been a certain ambiguity since the form, on the one hand, is supposed to be inherent in external things and, on the other hand, is also supposed to be comprehensible to the human mind, being something like an idea. Bacon now speaks of the "form of a nature" and says that "given the form the nature infallibly follows." Further, they are related such that the form "is always present when the nature is present, and universally implies it, and is constantly inherent in it." Again, "the Form is such, that if it be taken away the nature infallibly vanishes. Therefore it is always absent when the nature is absent, and implies its absence, and inheres in nothing else" (*ibid.*). Form and nature seem to be logically equivalent, but there is little doubt that Bacon intends some differentiation between them. He has in mind what was known in Scholastic times as the distinction between the "order of being" and the "order of knowledge." This distinction, or a very similar one, is implicit in the third book of Aristotle's *Metaphysics*, where he develops a parallel relationship between his "principles" and his "causes." Though the two are in one sense the same thing, the same form, they are found in two different realms: the causes are in the external world and the principles are in the realm of human discourse or cognition. The fact that the same form is supposed to be in each, that is, in the realm of being as well as in the realm of human cognition, makes possible knowledge of what really exists. In general, this is the basic epistemological theory of Aristotle and the Scholastics, and it appears that Bacon also adheres to it. Thus, when he speaks of a "nature" he means the form as it inheres in objects or relations in the external world. Although he usually refers to that form in the realm of human cognition as the "Form," in at least one passage he speaks of it as a "true definition" (aph. 20, p. 323). His usage of this term, also used by Aristotle, is an indication of Bacon's adherence to the Aristotelian epistemology. Further evidence for this point will be forthcoming when we analyze Bacon's application of his method to the "discovery of the form of heat."

This interpretation clarifies Bacon's belief that knowledge of the form somehow guarantees the ability to be able to reproduce the nature, that is, to "superinduce" the form upon other matter. This could only be possible if there were something identical in the knowledge of the form and the form inhering in matter. With this condition if one knew a true form there should be no problem at all in superinducing it upon other matter since what is known, the form, is the same thing as the nature one wishes to superinduce. Though the same form is in the mind as is in the external object, the two differ with respect to matter. The form as nature is combined with matter, whereas the form as true definition or principle is, presumably, uncombined with matter. When alchemists failed in an attempt to superinduce the form of gold upon the matter of some other substance, they attributed the failure either to their inadequate knowledge of the form or to the use of the wrong method of superinducing the form upon matter. They did not doubt the basic presupposition, the doctrine of forms which inhere in manner and are also supposed to be present in human cognition. Bacon is in this tradition and his doctrine of knowledge as power is much more an indication of his adherence to the Aristotelian epistemology than it is evidence that he was a precursor of modern pragmatism. He says that his "mode of operation," which seeks the form of simple natures, "proceeds from what in nature is constant and eternal and universal, and opens broad roads to human power, such as (in the present state of things) human thought can scarcely comprehend or anticipate" (aph. 5, p. 304). If Bacon meant by "forms" merely the "properties of things" in the sense of seventeenth-century mechanism, he would hardly describe them as constant, eternal, and universal. His occasional reference to them as laws is consistent with this description, for he speaks of the laws as "governing" and "constituting" the simple natures; what he has in mind is, essentially, some kind of hierarchy of forms ranked in terms of increasing generality. This conception of Bacon's completely misses the Galilean idea of measuring motion mathematically and ascribing the characteristics of things in the natural world to bodies in motion which efficiently cause them. This Galilean theory may properly be called "dynamic" since motion is the universal cause of all the properties of things. Bacon's conception is still essentially static; the universe for him consists of a number of simple forms or natures which constitute complex substances. These natures are ordered in a hierarchy of generality, natures like light, heat, or gravity forming part of the nature of a greater number of objects than the less general ones.

With the discovery of forms as the "mark of knowledge," Bacon proceeds to apply his method of "educing axioms from experience," which will enable us to discover the form. The first step is to prepare a natural and experimental history "ranged and presented in a suitable order," which he calls "Tables and Arrangements of Instances." Finally, the understanding must use induction in a "directed and guarded manner" in order to interpret the tables (aph. 10, p. 307). Bacon then proceeds to list twenty-seven "Instances Agreeing in the Nature of Heat," such as the rays of the sun, flame, and boiling liquids. Next he lists twenty-seven instances of a similar nature in which heat is absent. There is supposed to be a one-to-one correspondence between the items in each table with respect to one chief characteristic. Thus he opposes the instance of the rays of the moon, where heat is not present, to the instance of the rays of the sun, where heat is present. The two instances are similar in that both are about "rays from a heavenly body." Then he prepares a third table, this one of "Degrees or Comparison in Heat," in which he includes substances that have potential heat but not perceptible heat and also substances which are capable of great differences in intensity of heat.

With the completion of these three tables the work of "true induction" begins, and the first step is "the rejection or exclusion of the several natures which are not found in some instance where the given nature [heat] is present, or are found in some instance when the given nature is absent, or are found to increase in some instance when the given nature decreases, or to decrease when the given nature increases." This is easily said, Bacon remarks, but he admits that "the way to come at it is winding and intricate" (aph. 16, p. 320). This patient process of exclusion constitutes the core of Bacon's method, for it is at this point that he claims that his predecessors have gone wrong. When all the instances are listed, the natural inclination of the mind is to jump affirmatively to a generalization concerning the common "given nature" in all those instances. But what is most important, in Bacon's view, is that we should resist this inclination in favor of the negative method of excluding all the natures where the given nature (heat) does not occur, "at last to end in affirmatives, after exclusion has been exhausted" (aph. 15, p. 320).

The result of this process of "true induction" Bacon calls the "first vintage" or the "commencement of interpretation." The first point is that heat is a kind of action, for in every case where there is heat there is motion. He therefore concludes that motion is "as the genus of which heat is a species," and emphasizes that he means "not that heat generates action or that motion generates heat (though both are true in certain cases), but that *Heat itself its essence and quiddity, is Motion and nothing else.*" However, motion is limited by some "specific differences," which are: (1) "heat is an expansive motion, whereby a body strives to dilate and stretch itself to a larger sphere or dimension than it had previously occupied"; (2) heat is a motion "expansive or towards the circumference" and at the same time a "motion upwards"; (3) the expansive motion is not uniform to the whole body "but in the smaller parts of it"; and (4) the motion is rapid and "must proceed by particles, minute indeed, yet not the finest of all, but a degree larger." This, then, is the form, or as he now calls it, "the true definition," of heat.[18]

[18] *Ibid.*, aph. 20, p. 323. Emphasis supplied.

Later mechanistic philosophers, Hobbes, for example, account for phenomena like heat as subjective events that occur in connection with a sensing organism. Only bodies in motion exist externally, and these cause the heat but are not identified with it. Bacon not only refrains from utilizing this kind of theory but specifically denies it. He distinguishes sensible heat from the real nature of heat, calling the former a "relative notion" that has relation to man and not to the universe. Sensible heat, he remarks, "is correctly defined as merely the effect of heat on the animal spirits." He refuses to allow that a subjective element could be part of the essential nature of heat because sensible heat is variable "since the same body, according as the senses are predisposed induces a perception of cold as well as of heat" (*ibid.*). Real heat, in his view, must have a form which is eternal, constant, and universal and is not to be identified with what we sense.

It should be clear that the ultimate ontological element in Bacon's philosophy is, not the material body in motion or a material substratum, but the form. That he intends his forms to have the characteristics of eternality, universality, and simplicity should also be clear. However, we are left with his own insistence that he means something quite different from the meaning to which we have "hitherto been accustomed." What he wishes to deny here is that the forms are merely abstract ideas independent of matter. This seems to be little more than a rejection of the common interpretation of Platonism in which the "true realities of the universe" are supposed to be eternal ideas subsisting in an intelligible realm independent of the material world. Bacon allows that the forms have the characteristics that Plato ascribes to them, but insists on showing that they have an intimate and essential connection with matter. Left at this general a level, his position appears to be essentially an advance to Aristotelianism; however, there may be some original elements in Bacon's position. He says that the forms are "nothing more than those laws and determinations of absolute actuality, which govern and constitute any simple nature" (aph. 17, p. 320). So, he concludes, the form of heat is the same as the law of heat. Notice that Bacon does not draw a sharp distinction between the "law" and the "nature"; rather, the law constitutes the nature. This is not the same as the mechanical theory of mathematical laws governing the movements of bodies, in which there is a sharp distinction between the nature of the law and the nature of the body, the one being immaterial and universal and the other being material and particular. For Bacon "the form of a thing is the very thing itself, and the thing differs from the form in no otherwise than as the apparent differs from the real, or the external from the internal, or the thing in reference to man from the thing in reference to the universe" (aph. 13, p. 315). Here is a distinction, clearly enough, but it is not the "new" distinction of mechanical philosophy between mathematical laws, material atoms or particles, and observed properties. It is the "old" Aristotelian and Scholastic distinction of the order of being and the order of knowing. The two orders are supposed to be parallel and to share a common form; hence, we find Bacon identifying the form with the nature and with the true definition. Bacon apparently considers matter to be the carrier of the form, both limiting and containing it. This is evidently what he means when he speaks of matter as determining the form. Regardless of the status or role of matter, which is not perfectly clear, it is specifically distinguished from the form which is the object of knowledge.

At the beginning of this inquiry into Bacon's idea of metaphysics as the discovery of forms it was remarked that his early statements about the nature of forms, indicating their Aristotelian character, might not be consistent with his final position. After he developed his experimental method with its heavy emphasis upon detailed examination of sense observations, he might be expected to change his conception of the goal of knowledge into something more suitable to this method.

But it turns out that he was very careful to apply his method within the framework provided by his notion of the form as the object of inquiry. In the *De Augmentis*, published after both *The Advancement of Learning* and the *Novum Organum*, he consistently maintains his original position. There remains, then, in Bacon's philosophy a wide gulf between his conception of the goal of knowledge and the method that was to achieve it. One aspect looks to the past and is conceived in the framework of the Aristotelian metaphysics, while the other, the method, looks ahead to the development of natural philosophy in the seventeenth century in that it focuses attention on detailed sense observations. Bacon showed considerable ingenuity in developing his empirical method, which, though not actually used in the form he recommended, was inspirational to the English experimental philosophers in the generations following him. His conception of the goal of knowledge, however, showed hardly any development, having been derived with little change from the Aristotelian metaphysics. It is a mistake to suppose that Bacon had any conception of the nature of mechanical philosophy as it was later developed in mid-seventeenth century. His conception of the nature of natural philosophy was nonmathematical and well rooted in the Aristotelian formistic metaphysics.

Bacon failed to produce any important scientific discoveries by the application of his method and often did not recognize the good work of some of his contemporaries who used different methods. He criticized Gilbert for limiting himself to certain special phenomena, arguing that if one is to find the form of magnetism one must examine all the various instances of its occurrence since the form will be discovered as that which is common to them all. The general acceptance of Gilbert's theory indicated that sucess does not necessarily have to come from the comparison of all instances with each other but can come from an intensive examination of certain instances somehow recognized as the key ones. Bacon failed to recognize the possibilities of an intensive experimental method because of his metaphysics, his fixed idea that the goal of inquiry is an Aristotelian form that could only be discovered by examining all typical instances of its occurrence. Anything less than an examination of all instances would fail to reveal the common character, the form, and it would not be recognized. The fact that Bacon's method is quite different from the experimental method later developed by men like Hooke, Boyle, and Newton is further evidence that he was not a mechanistic philosopher.

Bacon's philosophy is deficient in all three basic elements of seventeenth-century mechanical philosophy. Although he praises Democritus and acknowledges that there are small particles of matter in things, he denies the "unchangeableness of matter" (aph. 8, p. 307). Even if it is granted that he has a minimum kind of atomism, he restricts matter to the subordinate role of the "carrier of the form." Matter may be the efficient cause of the observed properties of things, but beyond the matter is the real nature or the form. Though he has a notion of law, it is nothing like the mathematical law that is central to Newtonian mechanical philosophy.

The result of this explication of what Bacon meant by "metaphysics" is the discovery that Bacon may have been widely misinterpreted whenever he is called a "mechanical philosopher" or a precursor of the mechanical philosophy. One reason may be the failure to take seriously his definitions of "metaphysics" and "physics" in terms of the Aristotelian doctrine of causes. "Metaphysics" was, not just a token of respect to past authorities to appease the taste of his readers, but an integral part of Bacon's philosophy. It provides his conception of the nature of knowledge and reveals a mind well rooted in the Aristotelian formistic metaphysics.

CHAPTER 2

Metaphysics as the Definition
of Universal Terms

THOMAS HOBBES was the most prominent and influential English philosopher of the mid-seventeenth century, and it is to his thought that we now direct our attention. Our primary purpose is to determine his conception of metaphysics and explicate it in relation to his philosophy as a whole. Our secondary purpose is to analyze the relation between Hobbes's metaphysics and Bacon's modified Aristotelian metaphysics. It may be appropriate to deal with the latter topic first since both Bacon's and Hobbes's conceptions are developed in terms of the Aristotelian metaphysics, and this common reference point affords a convenient way of comparison.

The characteristically "mechanical" theory of atoms or particles of matter efficiently causing the observed properties of things is well developed in the thought of Thomas Hobbes. He wanted a complete break with the traditional metaphysics and rejected both formal and final causes, arguing that they were merely kinds of efficient cause. His position is almost a perfect reversal of Bacon's. The material and efficient causes which Bacon relegated to a subordinate status Hobbes elevated to the primary status of being the only kinds of causes. What Bacon thought of as the goal of scientific inquiry, the forms, Hobbes rejected as meaningless. What Bacon thought of as secondary objects of inquiry, important only in regard to their necessity as carriers or producers of the forms, the material and efficient causes, Hobbes regarded as the only legitimate objects of scientific inquiry. Since the theory of forms is the core of traditional metaphysics and Hobbes rejected forms as meaningless, it should be no surprise that his writings are full of strong disparaging remarks about metaphysics and metaphysicians. However, he reserves a legitimate task for metaphysics, namely, the "right limiting of universal significations."

"The writers of metaphysics," Hobbes remarks, "reckon up two other causes besides the *efficient* and *material,* namely the ESSENCE, which some call the *formal cause,* and the END, or *final cause;* both which are nevertheless efficient causes." [1] This turning from the formal cause to the efficient cause as the significant factor in the conception of reality and knowledge is one of the characteristic developments in seventeenth-century philosophical thought. Perhaps the greatest intellectual achievement of this period was the successful application of mathematics to natural philosophy by Galileo, Descartes, and Newton. The change in metaphysics is related to this development of mathematical natural philosophy. Mathematics is applied to motion, and motion in the physical world is efficient cause. Galileo's success in mathematically describing physical motion opened the way for the development of a science of mechanics. With this focus of attention on physical motion in the early seventeenth century, it should be expected that an attempt would be made to develop a metaphysics,

[1] *The English Works of Thomas Hobbes,* ed. Sir William Molesworth, 16 vols. (London: John Bohn, 1839–40), 1:131. Subsequent quotations are from this edition.

that is, an ontology and epistemology, around the conception of motion as efficient cause. Hobbes developed an ontology around the conception that matter (as innumerable small bodies) in motion (governed by the science of geometry, a physical science) efficiently causes our sense perceptions. This ontology is plausible and is even ingeniously worked out, but Hobbes has great difficulty with an epistemology to go with it. As part of his epistemological theory he allows a legitimate place for a science of metaphysics, or "prime philosophy" as he calls it. So, in order to evaluate this prime philosophy, we shall begin by explicating his epistemological theory.

Hobbes's stand against the Aristotelian metaphysics of formal cause affords a convenient introduction to his epistemological theory. He argues, "When it is said the essence of a thing is the cause thereof, *as to be rational is the cause of man*, it is not intelligible; for it is all one, as if it were said, *to be a man is the cause of man;* which is not well said" (1:131–32). Of course, to say the essence of a thing is its cause is unintelligible if one interprets "cause" as efficient cause. Except for the prime mover, a thing cannot cause itself efficiently and no one ever supposed it could. In this statement, "cause" clearly means formal cause and Hobbes's finding it unintelligible in terms of his own position is hardly an argument against the doctrine of forms. He has more to say, however, and remarks that "the knowledge of the essence of anything, is the cause of the knowledge of the thing itself; for if I first know that a thing is *rational*, I know from thence, that the same is a man; but this is no other than an efficient cause" (*ibid.*). He may be right here, for knowledge of something as a conception of the mind may efficiently cause further knowledge about the thing; at least, there is the evidence that the first conception precedes the second in time. Hobbes is satisfied to take this as conclusive evidence that he is dealing with efficient causation, although there is no experience of motion.

In Hobbes's example one has the idea that a thing is rational, and therefore, he says, one knows that the thing is a man. Whatever the relation is between these two ideas there does not seem to be any ground for describing it as a case of efficient causation. There is no actual motion; one idea does not cause the other to occur in anything like the sense in which one billiard ball striking another causes the second to move. It is very common to think of the activity of consciousness as a species of motion, but actually we are dealing with a metaphor. Hobbes has made up his mind, though, that the only reality is bodies in motion, and he is very much concerned with persuading his readers that the succession of ideas in the mind is a species of efficient causation, that is, a movement and, further, just the same kind of movement as physical bodies have.

The important point here is that Hobbes has turned the focus of attention from the ontological consideration of what is really in nature to the epistemological consideration of the succession of thoughts in the mind. Adherents of the doctrine of forms believed that the forms were real, that they existed in nature and not merely in the human mind. Hobbes affects to have no idea of such a possibility and assumes that the forms are supposed to be in the mind and only in the mind. He then argues that the relation between ideas in the mind is a species of efficient cause. This argument is not very good and even if it were it misses the point, that is, the issue of the status of the forms as existing in nature apart from the human mind as such. He offers no real arguments against this view but simply finds it unintelligible; he fails to understand his opponents' position (or pretends to) and resorts to ridicule.

Unable to offer direct arguments, Hobbes is doing something perhaps more significant. He is providing an alternative ontological and epistemological theory with the implied argument that his theory can handle the same problems more simply and, therefore, that the many distinctions of the traditional theory are unnecessary. Instead of the objects in nature being a combination of matter and form such that the essence of the thing (the form) is capable of being conceptualized in the human mind, he insists that only body or matter exists in nature. "The World, (I mean not the Earth onely, that denominates the Lovers of it *Worldly men*, but *the Universe*, that is, the whole masse of all things that are) is Corporeall, that is to say, Body; and hath the dimensions of Magnitude, namely, Length, Bredth, and Depth: also every part of Body, is likewise Body, and hath the like dimensions; and consequently every part of the Universe, is Body; and that which is not Body, is no part of the Universe: And because the Universe is All, that which is no part of it, is *Nothing;* and consequently *no where.*"[2] Body is "that which having no dependence upon our thought, is coincident or co-extended with some part of space."[3] The great variety of sensible qualities we experience is supposed to be really just bodies entering into different combinations because of their motion. "*Whatsoever accidents* or qualities our senses make us think there be in the *world,* they be *not* there, but are *seeming* and *apparitions* only: the things that really *are* in the world without us, are those *motions* by which these seemings are caused" (4:8). These accidents or qualities which we sense are no part of the natural thing; they are merely "*the manner by which any body is conceived,*" and the definition of an accident is "*that faculty of any body, by which it works in us a conception of itself*" (1:103).

The immediate object of sense perception as distinct from the independent external object is called a "phantasm." "Sense" is defined as "*a phantasm, made by the reaction and*

---

[2] Thomas Hobbes, *Leviathan* (1651; reprint ed., Oxford: Clarendon Press, 1909), chap. 46, p. 524. Subsequent quotations are from this edition.

[3] *Works of Thomas Hobbes*, 1:102.

endeavor outwards in the organ of sense, caused by an endeavor inwards from the object, remaining for some time more or less" (p. 391). This phantasm is located in the brain of the observer and does not exist externally, being merely "an *apparition* unto us of the *motion*, agitation, or alteration, which the *object* worketh in the *brain*, or spirits or some internal substance of the head" (4:4). Thus, what is finally perceived by the mind as an external object is not supposed to be anything like what really exists in nature except that it is some kind of body with three dimensions. All other characteristics, qualities or accidents, of perceived objects (with the additional exception of motion, evidently) are supposed to be, as he at different times calls them, "apparitions," "seeming," "fancy," or "phantasms." These terms connote unreality even though Hobbes defines "phantasm" as an actual motion in the brain. Further, as the immediate object of awareness, the phantasm can hardly be denied reality. Since it at least appears, it must be real in some sense. Hobbes has in mind a definite if perhaps limited meaning of "real" which can readily be deduced from his definition of "body" and his assertion (quoted above) that the universe is entirely composed of body. Body is coextended with some part of space and has no dependence upon our thought. If anything is real in Hobbes's philosophy it is body; and since body must not only be "coextended with some part of space" but also be independent of our thought, we can conclude that the core of his meaning of "real" is that which is independent of our thought. Phantasms, though they are located in our brains (hence, in space), depend upon our thought and, therefore, are not quite real.

If phantasms are unreal and qualitatively different from what is real, the external bodies in motion, then how is knowledge possible? It would seem that we could have no notion of the nature of external things since the phantasms are at least partially dependent upon our thought and do not present a likeness of what really exists externally. The answer is that since the external bodies in motion efficiently cause the phantasms, there is a relation of functional correspondence between the external cause and the phantasm. Thus, though the external real object may be completely different in nature from the phantasm, a change in the external object will produce a corresponding change in the phantasm. The phantasms then are functionally equivalent to their external causes, though they are qualitatively different in character. This answer goes beyond Hobbes's actual statements but is implicit in his theory.[4] It represents a conception of the nature of knowledge entirely different from the formistic Aristotelian theory. The development of this mechanistic theory of knowledge in philosophical thought following Hobbes is intimately related to the various conceptions of metaphysics we are primarily concerned with explicating.

The phantasms alone do not constitute knowledge, according to Hobbes; they are only a starting point. The experience of sense and memory is always particular, whereas "true knowledge" is always universal and consists in a perfect knowledge of causes. This universal knowledge is called "ratiocination" and is superior to the particular knowledge which consists in the phantasms. Hobbes, then, is interested, not in perception per se, but in knowledge of what causes perception. He defines "philosophy" as "the knowledge of effects or appearances, as we acquire by true ratiocination *from* the knowledge we have first of their causes or generation: And again, of such causes or generations as may be from knowing first their effects" (emphasis supplied). In this

---

[4] The same may be said of William of Ockham, who developed an extreme nominalism in opposition to the formistic theory of Thomas Aquinas. The theory of functional equivalence existing between external objects and human sense perception is suggested, or perhaps implicit, in Ockham's thought, though it is not clearly developed there.

definition he allows for the possibility of knowledge going both from appearances to causes and from causes to appearances. However, he immediately adds, "For the better understanding of which definition, we must consider, first, that although Sense and Memory of things, which are common to man and all living creatures, be knowledge, yet because they are given us immediately by nature, and not gotten by ratiocination, they are not philosophy." What he calls "philosophy" here is the preferred kind of knowledge since it is about causes and not merely about sense appearances, which nonrational animals also have. He defines "ratiocination" as computation, and "to compute, is either to collect the sum of many things that are added together, or to know what remains when one thing is taken out of another." Thus, it is a kind of adding and subtracting "in our silent thoughts, without the use of words" (1:3).

In ratiocination Hobbes maintains that an activity of reason comes forth, so to speak, from the mind to act upon the phantasms of sense. For example, he says that when we see a distant object obscurely, we have the idea of body; if we come nearer, we have the idea of a thing animated; and when we are nearer still and hear a voice, we have a third idea, of something rational. Lastly we "conceive" that all we have seen is one thing and we "compound" or "put together" these three ideas and get the idea of man (1:4). This is calculation or ratiocination, the adding or subtracting of ideas. In this simple illustration it would seem that each of the three ideas is supposed to come from the phantasm, for Hobbes says that we see something and then we have the idea, as if the thing seen produced it. This interpretation would allow the chain of efficient causation from the external object to be extended one step further and end, not in the phantasm, but in some general idea. Eventually, however, the mind must take the elements and "compound" them, that is, add these ideas and identify their sum with another idea. This process of ratiocination, which amounts to a process of identifying ideas with one another, is something quite different from the efficient causation of bodies in motion that produces the phantasm.

However, if the phantasm is supposed to produce the idea as the obscure thing at a distance would produce the idea of a body, why does Hobbes use the passive verb "have"? Why doesn't he say "produce" or "cause"? Probably, it is because he means that the mind already has the idea of body, for example, and recognizes the obscure thing as a body by noting an identical (not merely similar) element in the phantasm and in the idea. Concerning this interpretation the question arises about when and how the mind acquired the ideas it identifies with elements in phantasms. But Hobbes apparently was not interested in this question; he was concerned with the process in the rational mind, that is, in how it actually works, not in how it got the equipment it uses.

It is in examining the equipment necessary for ratiocination that we come to Hobbes's special conception of metaphysics. As we have seen he scornfully rejects the traditional (and Baconian) metaphysics of forms, and disparaging remarks about metaphysics and metaphysicians are common throughout his work. However, this attitude does not prevent him from reserving a legitimate role for a science of metaphysics. The examination of this conception will lead us back to this basic epistemological problem of the relation between the phantasms and the ideas which the mind compounds in order to come to a knowledge of the causes of things.

"There is a certain *philosophia prima*, on which all other philosophy ought to depend; and consisteth principally, in right limiting of the significations of such appelations or names, as are of all others the most universal." [5] These limitations of significations serve to avoid ambiguity and "equivocation

[5] *Leviathan*, chap. 46, p. 523.

in reasoning" and are called "definitions." Some of these universal terms are "body," "time," "place," and "motion," and they are "necessary to the explaining of a man's conceptions concerning the nature and generation of bodies." If there is any doubt that this discipline of constructing or limiting definitions is supposed to take the place of the metaphysics he has rejected, Hobbes himself remarks that it (his *philosophia prima*) "is commonly in the schools called *metaphysics*" and is a part of the philosophy of Aristotle which bears that title. The title, he says, has two senses: (1) that of the books placed after his natural philosophy or physics in compilations of his works and (2) the meaning the "schools" take, books of "supernatural philosophy." "And," he remarks, "indeed that which is there written, is for the most part so far from the possibility of being understood, and so repugnant to natural reason, that whosoever thinketh there is any thing understood by it, must needs think it supernatural" (chap. 2, p. 524). He leaves no room for doubt about his opinion of Aristotle and makes specific criticism of the theory of "substantial forms" or "separated essences" which he attributes to Aristotle.

Hobbes begins this criticism by asserting unequivocally his own position. "The world," that is, the universe or "the whole mass of all things that are," he affirms, "is corporeal, that is to say, body; and hath the dimensions of magnitude, namely, length, breadth, and depth . . . and that which is not body is no part of the universe" (*ibid.*). This statement alone would seem to be sufficient to eliminate "substantial forms" since these are not supposed to be corporeal. But Hobbes is interested in doing more than simply rejecting the traditional theory; he wants to locate whatever it was that that theory handled and to show his theory's ability to handle it, too. So, operating within his own conception of metaphysics, seeking the right signification or definition of words, he says, "To know now upon what grounds they say there be *essences abstract,* or *substantial forms, we are to consider what those words do properly signify"* (p. 525; emphasis supplied in the last phrase).

To find the definitions of words, it is first necessary to make clear just what words are and what uses they have. Words are signs and they are used "to register to ourselves, and make manifest to others the thoughts and conceptions of our minds. Words name different kinds of things or show the relationship between other names, and fall into four categories: (1) "the names of the things conceived; as the names of all sorts of bodies, that work upon the senses"; (2) "the names of the imaginations themselves" or the ideas or "mental images we have of all things we see"; (3) the names of names or "different sorts of speech" such as "universal," "plural," or "true" and "false"; and (4) words that "serve to show the consequence or repugnance of one name to another" (*ibid.*). The first three uses of words correspond to what might be called three different kinds of epistemological entities, things supposed to be real (different kinds of bodies), ideas or phantasms, and signs or words. The fourth use concerns the relations between words, and it is this use which is significant to the activity of reason, ratiocination, and the discovery of the "true causes of things." The relation between the real bodies and the appearances is efficient causation. The relation between the appearances or ideas and the words is signification.

For this fourth category of the use of words Hobbes considers the verb "to be" and its conjugations sufficient. Thus, his criticism of traditional metaphysical terms like "entity" and "essence" is that they are derived from the verb "to be" and "are therefore no names of things; but signs by which we make known that we conceive the consequence of one name or attribute to another" (p. 526). For example, when we say that "a man is a living body" we do not mean that "a man" is one thing, "a living body" another, and "is" a third, but merely that "man" and "living body" are the same thing. It should be clear from this example that although Hobbes speaks of showing the consequence or repugnance of one name to another, his remarks make no sense unless we take him to mean the consequence of what the names signify to one another. They signify "conceptions in our mind," and it is these conceptions which are added and subtracted and identified with other conceptions. It would be nonsense to say that the word "man" is the same thing as the words "living body." If there is any doubt about this point, one should remember the definition of ratiocination according to which it is a computation "in our silent thoughts, without the use of words." He conceives the essential process of reason to go on without words but grants that words greatly facilitate the process and make possible greater precision.

We are not principally concerned here with showing how Hobbes criticizes the doctrine of "Separated Essences," which he claims is "built on the vain philosophy of Aristotle." The main lines of his criticism naturally follow from his doctrine that the only reality is bodies in motion. If this is concurred with, then, of course, forms cannot be real. What we are concerned with is the interpretation he gives to the metaphysical terms of the traditional theory, "forms" or "essences." They signify "no thing" and consequently refer to nothing real, but they are legitimately signs "by which we make known that we conceive the consequence of one name or attribute to another" (*ibid.*). The Aristotelian theory of a parallel between the form in nature as the essence of a thing and the form in the mind as definition or quiddity is rejected by Hobbes (as it was by Ockham). But he allows in this theory something which corresponds to and serves the function of the form in the mind; this is the conception or idea which is named, that is, which is the referent of the name, when he speaks of showing the consequence of one name to another. These conceptions or ideas are not identified with forms in nature but simply with other ideas. However, he preserves the relation of identity as the crucial point in his epistemology. The verb "to be" is sufficient to show the consequences of ideas to one another: "Man is a rational animal" is a true statement because the idea signified by "man" and the idea signified by "rational animal" are "the same thing." Thus, Hobbes substitutes for the form a name which signifies an idea or conception, and the method of achieving knowledge of causes, what he calls "true knowledge," is the process of ratiocination, or identifying one idea with another.

The core of Hobbes's theory of knowledge is the process of ratiocination or the computation of ideas in the mind. It is a process of identifying ideas with one another and is the means by which universality is possible. Universality is the characteristic ingredient of philosophical knowledge and is never found in the phantasms themselves, which are always particular. For proper computation, ideas must be clearly defined and this is the task of prime philosophy, which replaces metaphysics. Given a series of phantasms, for example, it is necessary that we have in mind a definition of "man" before we recognize that a man is before us. That is, the definition, or "right limiting," of universal terms is supposed to come before successful ratiocination. This is why Hobbes calls this discipline "prime philosophy" and suggests that other sciences depend upon it. The adequacy of his theory of knowledge, then, depends upon the definitions, how they are arrived at, to what extent they are arbitrary, and to what extent they are real.

A definition is the "right limiting of a signification of a name," and a name is "a word taken at pleasure to serve for a mark, which may raise in our mind a thought like to some thought we had before, and which being pronounced to others may be to them a sign of what thought the speaker had, or had not before in his mind." [6] The process of ratiocination is carried on with conceptions or thoughts, and the words are used when communication is necessary. Names are "signs of our conceptions" and "they are not signs of the things themselves" (1:17). This conception in the mind is intermediary between the sign itself and the object in the external world. It is something like the natural sign in Ockham's theory, where the conception is functionally related to (and presumably produced by) the object in the external world. With Hobbes, as with Ockham before him, there need not be any qualitative similarity between the external object in nature and its conception in the mind. The conception may be merely a sign of the external object, but not an arbitrary sign. Hobbes brings out the nonarbitrary character of this relation very clearly by emphasizing the relation of efficient causation between external bodies in motion and the phantasm. The conceptions or ideas that our words signify are derived from the phantasms by a kind of abstraction. Phantasms are always particular and must be analyzed into parts which may be identified with parts of other phantasms in order to achieve generality. As parts of phantasms, then, the ideas or conceptions which are computed in the process of ratiocination are causally related to objects in the external world. An extreme nominalistic interpretation of Hobbes would attempt to eliminate the intermediary conception in the mind and reduce the elements of his theory to bodies in motion, phantasms, and words. This kind of interpretation is an oversimplification. Words are supposed to be instrumental and subordinate to the activity of reason; the computation of conceptions is possible without them. When Hobbes speaks of showing the consequence of one name to another he is not concerned with the name qua name or sign, which is a word of so many letters or a sound, but with the conception in the mind which is signified by the word.

[6] *Works of Thomas Hobbes*, 1:16.

Hobbes sometimes calls definitions "principles" or "primary propositions" and says that a definition is nothing but the resolution of a name into "its most universal parts." The definition of most names consists of giving their genus and difference. "But if any name be the most universal in its kind, then the definition of it cannot consist of *genus* and *difference*, but it is to be made by such circumlocution, as best explicateth the force of that name" (1:83). He formally defines "definition" as "*a proposition, whose predicate resolves the subject, when it may; and when it may not, it exemplifies the same*" (83–84). One of the properties [7] of a definition is that it gives a universal notion of the thing defined, which represents "a certain universal picture thereof, not to the eye, but to the mind" (p. 85). It is the explication of these universal notions that is the special task of prime philosophy. In defining a universal name it is necessary to resort to "circumlocution" to make the universal notion clear. Once the universal names are defined they may be used to construct a system of distinctions based upon genus and difference, which in turn may be used to define compounded (nonuniversal) names. As to the nature of these universal notions which are the basis of the universal names, we are given hardly a clue beyond the insistence that they do not admit of argument. They must be clear, that is, unless they are known by themselves they are not universal notions. If they are so clear and universal, they must be obvious to everyone. Hence this task assigned to

[7] There are seven: (1) it takes away equivocation and determines the signification of the defined name; (2) it gives a universal notion of the thing defined; (3) it exhibits so clear an idea of the thing defined that it is not necessary to dispute whether the definition be admitted or not; (4) definitions must be understood before compounded names can be understood; (5) compounded names may have different definitions depending upon context (as "hyperbole" has one definition in mathematics and another in rhetoric); (6) no name can be defined by any one word; and (7) a defined name ought not to be repeated in the definition.

prime philosophy must be a relatively simple one. It is necessary and very important in the sense that philosophy cannot proceed until it is performed, but Hobbes regarded it as a straightforward task involving few difficulties.

If Hobbes saw no special problems in regard to the nature of the universal notions or to the related question of their origin, many of his contemporaries and critics found here fruitful ground for controversy. The issue was between those who thought that universal notions could not be derived from external matter (and must, therefore, be innate in the mind) and those who believed they could only come from sense perception. These issues are well developed by the Cambridge Platonists, chiefly Ralph Cudworth and Henry More, and will be dealt with in a later chapter. They are mentioned now to indicate the direction of subsequent thought and to emphasize the continuity in the development of philosophical speculation related to conceptions of the nature of metaphysics. In the generation following the publication of Hobbes's major philosophical works (1651–56) the nature of universal notions and innate ideas became a major philosophical and religious issue.[8] Hobbes's *philosophia prima*, then, though he considered its task to be relatively minor, is related to one of the principal issues of seventeenth-century philosophical thought.

In explicating *philosophia prima* it has been necessary to outline Hobbes's epistemological theory. The definition of universal terms as the task of *philosophia prima* proves to be a necessary preliminary to philosophical knowledge. The universal terms are necessary for the formation of propositions which, in turn, are cast in syllogistic form for the ultimate purpose of drawing conclusions about the causes of natural phenomena. Hobbes's account of the actual process of achieving

[8] See John H. Yolton, *John Locke and the Way of Ideas* (London: Oxford University Press, 1956), pp. 26–48, for an excellent documentation of this development.

philosophical knowledge is markedly similar to the traditional Aristotelian method. His acceptance of both the Aristotelian logic of the syllogism and the method of definition by genus and difference makes this fairly clear. His rejection of Aristotle is based upon ontological rather than epistemological grounds. Hobbes was primarily concerned with establishing his theory of the nature of reality, the materialistic ontology of bodies in motion, and with discrediting the Aristotelian ontology whereby forms are supposed to subsist in the external world as the essences, or natures, of material things. He devoted less attention to epistemological problems, with the result that his philosophy could almost be characterized as a combination of a materialistic ontology and an Aristotelian epistemology. His retention of an essentially Aristotelian epistemology may, on the other hand, have been a matter of preference. Hobbes had no objection to the theory that forms are the content of the mind, provided that forms are interpreted as merely ideas or conceptions that have no subsistence outside the mind. All that was needed to combine this kind of theory of mind with the materialistic ontology was a plausible account of the relation between the external bodies in motion and the conceptions of the mind that are combined in propositions to constitute knowledge. Hobbes attempted to provide that account using the theory of efficient causation as a substitute when he rejected the traditional theory according to which this relation was qualitative similarity or identity. Knowledge is no longer conceived as providing a representation that is like or identical to the nature of reality; rather, it provides a representation which is functionally equivalent to and caused by external reality.

There are some important exceptions to this general theory which involve the concepts employed to describe and analyze the nature of body itself. Although Hobbes frequently and strongly asserts that what is immediately present to sense is seeming and fancy and corresponds only to "many several motions of the matter" in the external object, he could not intend for us to believe that body and motion are mere seeming and fancy. Surely we sense body and motion as parts of phantasms, and if these are seemings like colors and sounds and tastes, what are we to understand when he so strongly asserts that the universe is body and only body? It is impossible to read Hobbes and not realize that he understood all the conceptions which describe body (magnitude, figure, length, breadth, depth, etc.) as being real in the traditional sense. That is, in the case of conceptions of body (and also motion) the conception in the mind is supposed to be qualitatively similar to what exists in the real external world. With respect to these fundamental conceptions of body and motion, Hobbes's theory resembles the Aristotelian formistic theory. Each theory allows for a relation of qualitative similarity between the external reality and the conceptions of the mind. In Hobbes's theory, qualitative similarity is strictly limited, whereas it is general in the formistic theory. Hobbes's theory provides a simple, plausible conception of the nature of reality, whereas the formistic conception is complex and comparatively disorganized.

One of the rather large difficulties that results from Hobbes's combination of a materialistic ontology with an epistemology that contains many fundamental elements of the formistic theory is that a certain amount of equivocation is almost inevitable. He speaks of sensible qualities like sounds or colors or smells as a seeming or fancy which does not exist in external objects. They are supposed to actually consist in the "motion, agitation, or alteration, which the object worketh in the *brain*, or spirits or some internal substance of the head." [9] These motions of subtle matter in the head are supposed to be perfectly real since they are bodies in the universe. But they

[9] *Works of Thomas Hobbes*, 4:4.

are supposed to appear to our awareness in such ways that we have "apparitions" which are utterly unlike what exists externally. In one sense, then, the phantasms of sense are apparitions or seemings and, in another sense, they are "so many several motions of the matter." Actually there are two different categories, each of which has its own set of relations which have little meaning in the other. In the physical category the relation of efficient causation applies: bodies move and strike one another, and this is the only possible kind of cause since "motion produceth nothing but motion." In the other category, which includes phantasms, conceptions, and ratiocination, the principal relations are qualitative similarity and signification. Hobbes offers a theory of perception within the physical category, whereby sense is the result of an "endeavour" from the external object which meets a counterpressure or "outward endeavour" from the heart. The apparent externality of the phantasm is accounted for by this outward counterpressure of the human organs. Irrespective of its plausibility or merit, this theory is clearly ontological not epistemological; it offers an explanation of perception from the outside, so to speak, not the inside or the actual experience of sensing and thinking. This theory of perception as motion and countermotion of external bodies and subtler bodies in the brain is quite irrelevant to the epistemological problems of the actual method of obtaining philosophical knowledge. This method is described within a different category by using the elements of universal definitions, syllogisms, adding and subtracting of conceptions, and so forth. Hobbes does not even attempt to carry the physicalist category beyond the phantasms of sense. It is as if the chain of efficient causation ended with the phantasm, which, though it is what knowledge must begin with, cannot by itself ever constitute knowledge. The phantasms are particular, and philosophical knowledge is universal. This universality is achieved by analyzing the phantasms to derive conceptions which are common to other phantasms, and these conceptions are clarified by definition and then used to construct propositions. The operative relation involved in this process of phantasm analysis and definition formation is qualitative similarity. The mind recognizes similar elements in phantasms and forms general conceptions. The theory of bodies in motion, with its relation of efficient causation, has no place in the account of how universal knowledge is achieved.

Though the physicalist category and the category of conceptions, phantasms, and ratiocination are disparate, they are supposed to be related. The external bodies in motion produce or cause the phantasms, and the universal conceptions which are the elements of the final propositions of philosophical knowledge are derived from the phantasms. With respect to any single universal conception there is supposed to be a corresponding type of event in the external physical world, which is the source of the phantasm. The conception corresponds functionally to its cause in the external world, and in the case of some of the most basic conceptions there is a likeness as well, the idea of body being like real body. It seems possible to interpret Hobbes so that all likeness or qualitative similarity between conception and external object is denied. Functional correspondence (or signification) and physical causation would be the only relations obtaining between conception and external object. This type of theory is later developed by Locke, but it is incorrect to attribute such a theory to Hobbes. When Hobbes says that the universe is all body and only body, his words convey so strong a conviction that it is impossible to doubt that he believed that the conception of body was at least like or qualitatively similar to real or externally existent body. Nevertheless, the force of Hobbes's thought is definitely in the direction of emphasizing efficient causation rather than qualitative similarity as the ontological relation between the external object and the conception in the mind.

The explication of Hobbes's conception of metaphysics has led us into a lengthy discussion of his ontological theory and its relation to his theory of knowledge. This has been necessary for several reasons: his ontology of bodies in motion had to be outlined in order to discuss his rejection of the Aristotelian theory, and his epistemological theory had to be examined to make clear the task of his prime philosophy, which is part of his epistemology. Also, we have had to deal with the general metaphysical problem of the relation between the idea in the mind and the object in the external world. This problem provides the context for the conceptions of metaphysics explained thus far and for subsequent conceptions of metaphysics in the development of British empiricism.

CHAPTER 3

Metaphysics as Epistemological Theology

IN THE SECOND HALF of the seventeenth century, philosophers opposed to Thomas Hobbes's materialism took great interest in the question of how men come to have universal notions. The philosophers' interest in this particular issue was not merely a matter of intellectual curiosity nor merely a desire to explore all aspects of an issue; these men, of whom Henry More and Ralph Cudworth, the Cambridge Platonists, are outstanding examples, were interested in certain consequences they thought inevitable if all rational men share universal notions, such as, for example, cause and effect, whole and part, like and unlike, equality and inequality, and so forth. That there are such notions was popularly believed during the third quarter of the seventeenth century.[1] However, most believers in these notions and innate ideas were men concerned with defending the cause of religion. For this reason it is pertinent that Hobbes, the man who had the reputation for being the foremost English atheist of the seventeenth century, also accepted the doctrine of universal notions. When an atheist accepted this doctrine, men like Cudworth and More rejoiced in their conviction that they could prove that the Supreme

[1] Yolton, *John Locke and the Way of Ideas*, pp. 27–47.

Being exists as the origin of the universal notions. They attempted to show that these notions could have no source other than a Supreme Being.

Henry More develops the issue more clearly than Cudworth. In a polemic against atheism More uses some of the traditional arguments for God's existence, but they are fitted into the framework of a basic innate-idea argument. He begins by recommending that we not *"judge of the truth of any Proposition till we have a settled and determinate apprehension of the terms thereof."* [2] This approach is consistent with Hobbes's definition of *"philosophia prima."* It is also similar to Principle X, in which Descartes observes that "before we can ever understand the meaning of 'I think, therefore, I am' . . . we must first of all know what is knowledge, what is existence, and what is certainty." Descartes does not make this simply a matter of definition and even remarks that "philosophers err in trying to explain by definitions logically constructed, things which were perfectly simple in themselves." [3] Rather, it is a matter of having "notions of the simplest possible kind" ready in mind. He even suggests that such notions are "inborn in us," though he does not develop this point. Both Hobbes and Descartes maintain that the notions are fundamental to knowledge, but do not offer accounts of their origin. They apparently assumed that all men accepted these notions as far as meaning and content were concerned, and neither saw any reason to discuss them further.

The next move in this line of thought is to focus attention on the origin of these universal notions. This is done most clearly by More, but Cudworth and others emphasize the same

[2] Henry More, *An Antidote against Atheism*, in *A Collection of Several Philosophical Writings*, 4th ed. (London: Joseph Downing, 1711), p. vii. Subsequent quotations are from this edition.

[3] René Descartes, *The Principles of Philosophy*, in *The Philosophical Works of Descartes*, trans. Elizabeth S. Haldane and G. R. T. Ross, 2 vols. (Cambridge: Cambridge University Press, 1911), 1: 222.

thing. More speaks of a principle that is "more noble and inward than reason itself" and upon which reason depends. He calls it "Divine Sagacity" and asserts that "the beginnings of Reason is not Reason, but something which is better," and immediately suggests that this can only be God.[4] In broad outline this is the strategy of *An Antidote against Atheism*. More shows that reason depends upon some special intuitive faculty for its universal notions, which, he argues, are more basic than reason itself since they come first. When he thinks he has established this point, he proceeds to argue that the source of notions, as well as of the Divine Sagacity which produces them, can only be God. To establish his argument, More must first refute the Hobbesian or "atheistical" position that the notions must come from matter. If any valid reasoning is possible, the argument goes, God must exist as the source of the universal notions upon which reasoning depends. And More was confident that his strongest opponent among the atheists, Hobbes, did in fact share his belief in the validity of reason.

More's doctrine of innate ideas, if one may call it that, is quite different from the universal notions of Descartes and Hobbes. They considered the notions to be more or less fixed; that is, the universal notion is what is defined in a definition, or the meaning of a definition. More has in mind a faculty or activity as distinguished from fixed notions. The reason for this should be clear if we keep in mind his general strategy. He emphasizes activity because he is looking to the origin of the notions rather than at the character of the notions themselves and how they function in reasoning. He thinks of origin in terms of creation or making and postulates an active faculty which creates these universal notions.

More's emphasis upon the active faculty which creates universal notions is somewhat puzzling when we consider that

[4] *Antidote against Atheism*, p. vii.

his avowed purpose in writing is to enhance the conception of the power of the Creator and to provide arguments and evidence for his existence. If the mind has the power to create universal notions why invoke God to do the job? It is not immediately clear why More was not satisfied with the theory that God placed or implanted these ideas in human minds. Descartes and Augustine as well as many minor writers of More's period were satisfied with this picture.[5] Descartes in the "Third Meditation" speaks of the idea of God in our minds as being "like the mark of the workman imprinted on his work."[6] This metaphor emphasizes the fixed character of the notions, for what is printed is as definite or determined as a word upon a page. How these conceptions are actually created is left to the Deity; we are simply supposed to find them fixed in our minds. Perhaps More was aware of the somewhat oversimplified nature of this theory. It is open to the immediate objection that not everyone finds these innate universal notions present in his mind; or one could wonder why they are not present in the minds of young children since the thoughts are supposed to be inborn. There are many similar obvious objections to the naïve innate-idea theory[7] that More may be trying to meet with a more sophisticated theory.

More's chief targets are atheism and the philosophical theories that support it. Hobbes's materialism is one of the most prominent of these; it provided a philosophical basis for atheism in the sense that it made God unnecessary for the account of how we obtain knowledge. The universal notions must be derived from matter since it is all that exists externally, and More felt that this derivation must be a passive

[5] Yolton, *John Locke and the Way of Ideas*, pp. 30–48.

[6] Descartes, *Philosophy*, 1 : 170.

[7] These are set forth in Book 1 of John Locke's *An Essay concerning Human Understanding*, collated and annotated, with prolegomena, by Alexander Campbell Fraser, 2 vols. (New York: Dover Publications, 1959).

process. External objects as bodies in motion produce the phantasms of sense in a mechanical manner, and since all universal notions are derived from the phantasms, these notions are also mechanical productions of matter. God is no part of this process in Hobbes's account; and in order to develop a countertheory in which God plays a role, More emphasizes the activity of reason in the knowing process, rather than the mechanical process of bodies in motion producing phantasms of sense. More felt that the activity of the mind or reason was more akin to the spiritual nature of the Deity than to the mechanical action of material bodies. The mind is active in the sense that it wills, selects or chooses, and initiates the movements of the material body. Matter or body is passive in the sense that it does none of these things; it is what is acted upon. The naïve innate-idea theory, whereby the idea is imprinted in the mind by God, bore an uncomfortable resemblance (for a religious mind) to the materialistic account, which contends that external matter produces the idea. In each case the human mind is passive with respect to an external cause. There is the suggestion, then, that More emphasized the activity of the human mind in his account of the knowing process in order to distinguish his theory as sharply as possible from the materialistic theory. The general point (to be discussed in detail later) is that he wished to associate activity with mind, reason, and the Deity, and to associate passivity with matter or body. He must then argue that activity and not passivity is the essential characteristic of philosophical knowledge.

Let us now look at More's argument more closely. He begins by claiming to prove the existence of God from the one postulate, "that our faculties are true." He does not get his arguments from books "but fetch'd them from the very nature of the thing itself . . . indelible *ideas* of the Soul of man," [8]

---

[8] *Antidote against Atheism*, Preface, p. 3.

or as he later says, from the "innate properties" of the "Mind of Man" (p. 5). But, he argues, these properties must be guaranteed in some way since the most obvious examples of pure mental activity (such as mathematical thinking) may be just delusional peculiarities of human minds. For More as for Descartes, a good God is this guarantee.

There are two ways of using innate ideas to argue for God's existence. The first, the one just outlined, is the more ambitious. It begins with some clear and distinct ideas which may plausibly be called a priori since they are not obviously drawn directly from experience, and then proceeds to the conclusion that they could have no source other than a Divine Being. This argument is ambitious because, starting from a premise that is likely to gain acceptance by all parties, it aims to convince everyone; at least this was likely in the seventeenth century, before Locke's *Essay*. The second way is the Cartesian way, which begins with the postulate that there is a clear, indubitable idea of God in the minds of all men. The procedure is then to argue that such an idea could not have come to the mind in any way other than by divine cause. This way of arguing is less ambitious since it convinces only those who already admit to having the idea of God in their minds. The large majority of the people in the seventeenth century probably had this preconceived idea, though logically there was nothing to prevent their doubting its validity. Skeptics and atheists need not have acknowledged that they had any such clear innate idea in their minds, though they were usually obliged to admit that they knew what the word "God" meant. Regardless of whether atheists had a clear innate idea or merely knew the meaning of the word, they were just as anxious as the believers to admit that there are universal notions. Since both atheists and the defenders of religion believed in reason, the best way to convince an atheist would have been to begin with a single postulate which he could accept, namely, "that our faculties are true." Though More uses the less effective second way of arguing, he places greater emphasis upon the first, and it is to this that we will direct our attention.

More suggests that just as we accept matter as the cause of our sense impressions so we ought to accept spirit as the cause of the innate ideas or universal notions we find in our minds. Though he admits that matter is the cause of sense perception, he regards reason and the universal notions as more significant in the production of knowledge. Sense perception, he argues, requires the active mind before it becomes meaningful; and matter, as merely the first impulse, is relegated to minor status. He asserts that "there is an active and *actual knowledge* in a man, of which these outward objects of sense are rather the reminders than the first Begetters or Implanters." He continues:

When I say actual knowledge, I do not mean there is a certain Number of *Ideas* flaring and shining to the *Animadversive Faculty*, like so many *Torches* or *Stars* in the *Firmament* to outward sight, that there are any *Figures* there, like the *Red Letters* or *Astronomical Characters* in an *Almanack*. But I understand thereby an active sagacity of the soul, or quick recollection, as it were, whereby some small Business being hinted upon her, she runs out presently into a more clear and larger conception. [P. 17]

The influence of the Platonic theory of recollection is evident from this passage. The objects of sense are reminders and this actual knowledge is a kind of quick recollection. The Platonic theory itself, however, deals with fixed and determinate ideas which bear resemblance to their archetypes in the Platonic heaven of Ideas. More, on the other hand, is concerned with this active sagacity which produces the ideas, the fixed character of the ideas being underemphasized in favor of the active creative power of the mind. More's theory may be called a doctrine of *potentially present innate ideas.* They are innate since he denies that they come from experience in the sense of external bodies in motion being their cause. They are potential since he denies that they are always present in the mind as fixed entities. They are rather something the mind is capable of producing as it does ideas of imagination, but in the case of the innate ideas there is not supposed to be any arbitrariness. For, despite the fact that More denies that the ideas are always present in the mind as fixed entities, he maintains that they are nevertheless objectively valid in the manner of Platonic Ideas. But they are not simply in the mind, available for ready and easy reference; effort, inclination, and creative power are required for the mind to reproduce or apprehend these ideas.

More provides an analogy which helps to clarify his meaning. The mind of a sleeping musician does not "so much as dream anything concerning his Musical Faculty, so that in one sense there is no *actual skill* or Notion, nor representation of any thing Musical in him." However, if a friend awakens him and asks him to perform, perhaps "telling him two or three Words of the beginning of the Song," the musician will presently sing the song beautifully. Just so, says More,

> the mind of Man being jogg'd and awakened by the impulses of outward objects, is stirred up into a more full and clear conception of what was but imperfectly hinted to her from external occasions; and this Faculty I venture to call *actual knowledge,* in such a sense as the sleeping Musician's skill might be called *actual skill* when he thought nothing of it. [*Ibid.*]

He has chosen an analogy, not to some instance of recalling a fixed idea as Plato does in the *Phaedo* with the idea of perfect equality, but to a skill, a knowing how rather than a knowing that. This analogy also brings out what he has in mind when he insists on referring to this faculty or sagacity of the mind as an "actual knowledge." Calling it "actual" when it is not in operation and producing an idea in present consciousness seems odd and unjustified; one would think the term "potential" more appropriate. Evidently, however, "potential" is too weak for More's meaning, and why this is so becomes evident if we look closely at the analogy. If More had called the sleeping musician's skill "potential," it would not be distinguished from the skill anyone else could acquire with training and practice. This latter, hypothetical skill would be properly potential in the sense that any man with a good ear and nimble fingers is potentially a good pianist. So, following More's line of thought, the skill of the already trained and practicing musician when he is asleep could not be called merely "potential." Therefore, More calls it "actual knowledge" in the sense of a skill or faculty that is possessed but not always in operation.

On one hand, More would have the universal notions to be not just fixed entities that are taken out of a drawer, so to speak, when needed, but entities that are creatable by an active power of the mind. He wishes to emphasize the activity of mind in the knowing process so that he can deemphasize the role of external matter as the cause of sense impressions. On the other hand, he wishes to retain the advantages of the naïve theory, that is, that the universal notions have objective validity in the sense that they are the same for all men and are the basis of human reason. This objective validity, the fixed character of the universal notions, is essential if those notions are to be the basis of reason. The creative aspect, the activity of mind required for their production, is necessary for More's point of view in order to discredit the materialistic theory that they have their origin in matter.

It is not enough for More to make a plausible case for the theory that universal notions are potentially present in the mind and are capable of being called forth when they are "hinted at"; he also has to show that they "could not have been impressed from without." More does not think that he must expend much effort on this point and simply observes that "they are no sensible nor physical affection of the Matter." If only bodies in motion exist externally, as Hobbes claims, then only such affections as size and shape could be directly caused by matter. The universal notions do not qualify as sensible or physical affections of bodies in motion, as Hobbes himself would agree. More then asks, "How can that which is no physical affection of the matter, affect our corporeal organs of sense?" No answer is forthcoming, of course, and More concludes that it "necessarily follows" that since the universal notions could not come from without, "they are from the soul herself within, and are the Natural Furniture of Human Understanding" (p. 18).

More's next step, now that he has located the origin of the universal notions in the active sagacity of the mind, is to use this point to reenforce the more familiar innate-idea argument for the existence of God. He maintains that he has sufficiently demonstrated that:

> the *Notion* or *Idea* of *God* is as *natural, necessary* and *essential* to the Soul of Man, as any other *Notion* or *Idea* whatsoever, and is no more *Arbitrarious* or *Fictitious* than the Notion of a *Cube* or *Tetraedrum*, or any other of the Regular Bodies in Geometry which are not devised at our own pleasure. [P. 21]

Notice that the criterion for necessary ideas is that they are not subject to our pleasure or arbitrary whim. Ideas such as the axioms of geometry must be accepted, and More claims that the idea of God is in the same category. The reasons why we are supposed to have no choice but to entertain the idea of God in our minds are not the same as those for axioms of geometry, however. Axioms of geometry are clear, distinct, and immediately evident when they are comprehended but this is not the case with the idea of God. As More has been at pains to argue, the idea of God is "necessary" to the mind because the universal notions which are clear in themselves cannot come from external matter. Therefore, he reasons, they must be natural to the mind, that is, come from the mind itself; and, since the mind is spirit, as God is spirit, the original source must be the Deity. This is an argument and not an instance of noticing certain characteristics of ideas. Universal notions and the axioms of geometry have a certain simplicity and ready comprehensibility which is certainly not the case with the idea of God. More himself occasionally seems to realize this. From the point of view of simplicity and clarity, the idea of God is nothing like the axiom that a straight line is the shortest distance between two points.

More makes a mistake in putting the idea of God on the same level as the other universal notions. The idea of God does not have the characteristics or the function of the universal notions, which are supposed to be the basis, or starting point, that reason requires in order to operate. The idea of God is certainly not necessary for the functioning of human reason, as evidenced by atheists, who reason perfectly well without it and might deny that they find the idea innately in their minds. Therefore it would not be a universal notion, and in maintaining that it is, More shows an excess of zeal. Thinking that his basic contention is established, More tries to give it greater force by tying it in with the Cartesian argument. That argument proceeds from a characteristic of the idea of God— perfection—but More's theory proceeds from the necessity of universal notions fulfilling the function of making reason possible. God's existence is proved indirectly in More's argument since God is supposed to be the only possible cause of universal notions in the human mind. More not only weakens his argument by attempting to associate it with the quite different Cartesian stand but also causes confusion and loses the accord of atheists on the acceptance of universal notions as common ground (an atheist would hardly accept a set of universal notions including the idea of God). More's own epistemological argument is adequate for his purpose, though this adequacy depends upon the acceptance of a presupposition regarding the nature of spirit.

This presupposition is that the activity of the human mind is understood to be the same as the activity of the divine spirit, the human mind being either a creation of the divine spirit or, in a mystical sense, a part of that spirit. The universal notions then, since they are a product of the activity of the human mind, depend upon or are an ultimate product of the divine spirit. What novelty there is in this argument for the existence of God stems from the conception of mind as spirit in a mystical and divine sense. This is mystical in the sense of Plotinus and the neo-Platonists who were well known to both Cudworth and More. What More uses from this tradition are the emphasis upon the active creative power of mind in the knowing process and the conception of mind as spirit, spirit being understood as divine. From this point of view the question concerning the origin of the universal notions seems to have an obvious answer. Their source is in the activity of mind, and since this activity is considered divine in character, the general lines of More's argument for the existence of God are clear. However, when one does not think in the context of More's neo-Platonic presupposition that mind is divine spiritual activity, his argument is weak. Denying that mind is divine, even an atheist could happily admit that universal notions come from the activity of mind and not from matter. He need only observe that such notions are produced by the activity of mind, as More argues, and then deny that there is anything divine about the activity. Plausible as this line of reasoning may seem, it apparently did not occur to More or his contemporaries. Thinkers accustomed to the Cartesian dualism of mind and matter found the idea that the mind was akin to the nature of the divine quite believable. Both atheists and divines were confident that the nature of God is certainly not material, and that if there are only the two substances conceivable to human reason, then there is a natural presumption that the divine nature is more like mind than matter. Since More was both a Cartesian and a man of religious conviction, he quite naturally presupposed that the activity of the human mind was of the same nature as the activity of divine spirit.

We have discussed More's argument for the existence of God from the universal notions of the mind and have called this an "epistemological" argument. Not usually so classified, More, and also Cudworth, are in the line of development of British empiricism. Although one commentator was correct for the most part in remarking that it was as part of the mystical tradition of Plotinus "rather than in the epistemological development of English philosophy, that More's thought finds its place,"[9] it is a mistake to suppose that there is no place for Henry More in the development of British epistemological thought. He takes up the epistemological problem of the origin of universals where Hobbes left it, and advances a solution which is at least in the right direction since it emphasizes the activity of mind. Of course, we might say that in general his motivation involves a desire to defend religious beliefs and the content of his thought derives from the mystical tradition in philosophy.

This is not the only time the mystical tradition entered into the development of British empiricism: it influenced Berkeley in much the same way, and he, too, was motivated by a desire to defend religious beliefs. Though a discussion of Berkeley would be premature at this time, the usage of the terms "idea" and "notion" by him and by More should be

[9] Flora Isabel Mackinnon, *Philosophical Writings of Henry More* (New York: Oxford University Press, 1925), p. xix.

mentioned now. More sometimes uses them synonymously and sometimes not, so that one wonders just what distinction, if any, he intends to mark. Also, he uses "idea" and "image" synonymously but never "notion" and "image." It would seem, then, that "idea" is used when a conception is simple and clear, with the visual image as the standard case. "Notion" seems to be used in cases where there is some kind of complexity or where the conception is not something that can be visualized. However, notions are not necessarily supposed to be unclear. They may be just as clear and simple as visual images, the notion of equality being such a case. There is, however, considerable fluctuation concerning the standard for simplicity and clarity; sometimes it is the easily grasped abstract or mathematical ideas like equality and sometimes it is the visual image. More uses "idea" when he wants to suggest the maximum of clarity in a conception. This is why, for example, he speaks more often of the "Idea of God" than of the "Notion of God." Since there is no image of God and since the conception is not abstractly simple, he ought to speak of the "Notion of God," as does Berkeley. Calling this conception an "idea" may be a persuasive device to set it apart from the universal notions in an attempt to exalt it and suggest greater clarity and simplicity than is there. Like More, Berkeley uses both terms, "notion" and "idea," but is consistent where More is not. Berkeley uses "notion" to denote conceptions in which there is never a particular image, the conception being about spirit or the activity of spirit. He uses "idea" to denote a particular sensible image. A foretaste of Berkeley's distinction is present in More's discussion, but the ambiguity so prevalent in More, and also in Locke, is eliminated in Berkeley's thought.

We were led into this discussion of More's argument for the existence of God by following up the issue of universal notions that were the legitimate concern of Hobbes's prime philosophy. Hobbes and Descartes showed little interest in the origin of these notions, though Descartes did maintain that they were innate. We looked next to More because he, along with Cudworth, was one of the most prominent critics of Hobbes in the seventeenth century. More was very much interested in the origin of the universal notions, so much so that it was this issue which led him to develop from innate ideas a somewhat novel proof of the existence of God. This may seem a rather slender thread to follow when one is trying to find out just what metaphysics was supposed to be. However, it leads directly to a basic conception of metaphysics for the seventeenth-century British philosophers and also to a conception which carries over to the next century and the main line of epistemological thought.

In approaching this basic conception of metaphysics let us notice some of the ways More speaks of it and metaphysicians. He frequently uses "theological" as a synonym for "metaphysical," so a first approximation of what More means by "metaphysics" would be simply theology. This subject would consist chiefly of arguments for the existence of God, the basis of these being More's doctrine of potentially present innate ideas. However, this tie-in of epistemological considerations with theology indicates a more general meaning, too. Throughout a discussion of the history of philosophy, More constantly employs a dichotomy between what he calls the "physical or Mechanical" and the "Theological or Metaphysical." [10] Or, as in the following passage, he contrasts "metaphysicians" and "Atomical Philosophers":

The metaphysicians [are] growing vain in spinning out needless and useless subtitles, ridiculous falsities concerning immaterial beings, for want of some other objects to exercise their Reason upon; and the Atomical Philosophers [are] becoming over-

[10] *Antidote against Atheism*, p. xvii.

credulous of the powers of Matter; nay, I may say, too too impious and impudent in exploding the belief of *Immaterial Beings*, in condemning the Rules and Maxims of *Virtue* and *Morality*. [P. xix]

Notice that the "metaphysicians" are supposed to be concerned with immaterial things, while the "Atomical Philosophers" are supposed to be concerned with material or physical things. What we have here is the Cartesian dualism of mind and matter, with the inquiry into mind or immaterial things being called "metaphysics," while the inquiry into matter or physical things is called "Atomical" or "mechanical" philosophy. Also, again using a similar distinction, we find More remarking that he admires Descartes's "mechanical wit" but adds that he "might be no master of Metaphysics to me" (p. 3). The general meaning of metaphysics, then, is that it is the study of mind and what relates to it, whereas mechanical or atomical philosophy is the study of matter and its workings.

To clarify this basic conception of metaphysics, we might now attempt to gather some of the strands that have been worked so far and look for a pattern of what metaphysics was supposed to be. In the original Aristotelian version there were three ways of viewing metaphysics: as the science of first principles, as the science of being qua being, and as theology, the science of the divine. Roughly, the first way is epistemological, the second is ontological, and the third is, of course, theological. All three are closely interrelated since the ultimate first principle is also a cause; it is the prime mover or God. This prime mover is pure, fully actualized form, and form turns out to be the essential ingredient of being. In the natural world only particular substances are supposed to exist, and these are always a union of form and matter; however, little can be said of matter itself except that it is the principle of potentiality and individuation. But potentiality, as such, is understood as the coming to be of actuality, which is form, so that not only is it impossible for pure matter to exist alone but it is incomprehensible without some form. It is with this conception of form that traditional Aristotelian metaphysics unites its component parts, for the principles or causes are forms which are at once the essential part of being, that is, what exists, and they are also what is knowable to the human mind by somehow being realized in it. Thus knowledge becomes the realizing in mind of the form, which is the essential part of what exists outside mind. The theological aspect is tied in by the theory of pure form, or perfect actuality or form without matter, which is the divine prime mover. This prime mover, in turn, causes movement (the process from potentiality to actuality) by attracting, that is, by being the end or purpose.

This summary of Aristotelian metaphysics is rather general, but to have some reminder of the traditional theory before us is necessary if we are to understand what happened to metaphysics from the time of Bacon on into the eighteenth century. The potentiality-actuality principle served to integrate the three aspects of the Aristotelian metaphysics. By abandoning it Bacon separated theology from epistemology and ontology, for the theory of pure form as divine is plausible only in connection with the concept of form mixed with matter in a state of potentiality. Bacon was then free to use Aristotle's four causes to classify physics and metaphysics since the causes are no longer integrated by the principle of potentiality-actuality. Further, the removal of final causes from physics may be understood in relation to the abandonment of the potentiality-actuality principle. For, if motion is regarded as simply change of place rather than as a process of development from potentiality to actuality, then the final cause, the actuality to be achieved, is no longer needed to explain motion and may be safely dropped from physics.

However, Bacon specifically limited the science of physics to material and efficient causes, which he subordinated to the formal cause, the proper object of knowledge. He used elements from two entirely different ontologies, the Democritean theory of motion and the Aristotelian theory of forms, and failed to integrate them. He gave no account of how bodies in motion are supposed to be related to forms. In the traditional theory, matter was not regarded as anything positive in itself but only as a principle of potentiality which made change possible. Matter was a mere evidence that a form was in process of realization. When the potentiality-actuality principle is eliminated, however, and a theory of matter as bodies in motion in a void is substituted, it becomes extremely difficult, if not impossible, to construct a plausible theory about the relation between matter and form.

More interpreted metaphysics as the study of the immaterial, and mechanical philosophy as the science of the material. Neither he nor Cudworth took issue with the materialistic ontology in the sense of doubting that bodies in motion exist or that these constitute the external world. Granting the strictly ontological issue, More shifted the focus of attention to that of epistemology. Hobbes's materialistic ontology remained dominant until it was later challenged by Berkeley. The three aspects of Aristotelian metaphysics were reduced to theology and epistemology, which were integrated by More with the concept of the immaterial or spiritual or divine. Thus metaphysics as the science of the immaterial included two kinds of problems, epistemological and theological, and was contrasted with natural philosophy, which supplants ontology and deals with the material world.

CHAPTER 4

Metaphysics and the Doctrine
of Innate Ideas

To HENRY MORE metaphysics emerged as a combination of theology and epistemology—a combination effected by means of a version of the innate-idea doctrine. Other men related the same doctrine to different issues, all closely associated with conceptions of the nature of metaphysics. Ralph Cudworth was among those who connected the doctrine with the issue of the status of traditional moral and religious beliefs and feared that the new science, with its emphasis upon the material universe, was subversive to those beliefs. Another group, including Isaac Barrow, friend and teacher of Newton, associated the doctrine with the development of Newtonian natural philosophy. However, not all philosophers were so approbative in their views concerning the innate-idea doctrine as Barrow and Cudworth. Notable among the latter group was John Locke, whose famous polemic against the doctrine will be discussed in detail.

Ralph Cudworth was perhaps the best known and most influential of the Cambridge Platonists, with the possible exception of Henry More. Their theories of innate ideas are similar, but the influence of Aristotle is more evident in Cudworth's thought. He maintains that "knowledge and intellection doth not merely *prospicere*, look out upon a thing at a distance, but makes an inward reflection upon the thing it knows and . . . reads inward characters written within itself, and intellectually comprehends its object within itself, and is the same with it." [1] He then quotes Aristotle as saying that in abstract things which are the objects of science "the intellect and the thing known are really one and the same." But Cudworth adds, "Those ideas or objects of intellection are nothing else but modifications of the mind itself" (*ibid.*). This is an appeal to the traditional Aristotelian epistemology, according to which the form, the object of knowledge, is the essence of the external object and is also realized in the mind. However, Cudworth gives these "objects of intellection," or forms, a somewhat mentalistic cast, emphasizing their aspect as objects in or modifications of the mind. Aristotle emphasized the objective or natural aspect of the form as the essence of external things in the natural world. To Cudworth as it is to Henry More, this emphasis upon mind as opposed to the external material world as the source of knowledge is a reaction to the materialism of Hobbes.

Cudworth even tries to deny the significance of perception since it is supposed to be efficiently caused by external bodies in motion. "Sense" he maintains, "is but the offering or presenting of some object to the mind, to give it an occasion to exercise its own inward activity upon" (p. 564). It is "a slight and superficial perception of the outside and accidentals of a corporeal substance" and does not, he insists, "penetrate into the profoundity or 'inward essence' of a thing" (p. 565). It is the mind, Cudworth believes, that does penetrate to the "inward

---

[1] Ralph Cudworth, *The True Intellectual System of the Universe*, trans. J. Harrison, 3 vols. (London, 1845), 3:566. Subsequent quotations are from this edition.

essence" because the mind is either one with or of the same nature as the essence of the natural object. Lest it be felt that this interpretation of traditional epistemological theory is excessively mystical, we should be reminded of the position of Aristotle, who says that thought

> shares the nature of the object of thought; for it becomes an object of thought in coming into contact with and thinking its objects, so that *thought and object are the same.* For that which is capable of receiving the object of thought, i.e., the essence, is thought.[2]

Cudworth adheres to this Aristotelian theory, but he does so with a vigorous emphasis on the activity of mind. "For knowledge is not a knock or thrust from without," he remarks, "but it consisteth in the awakening and exciting of the inward active powers of the mind." [3]

Cudworth employs the same kind of active innate-idea theory as More in the defense of moral and religious values. He attempts to develop a doctrine of maxims about these innate values, which, since they are inborn in the mind, are justified independently of the senses and the material universe. He remarks, however, that he has

> not taken all these pains only to confute scepticism or fanaticism, or merely to defend and corroborate our argument for the immutable natures of just and unjust; but also for some other weighty purposes that are very much conducing to the business that we have in hand. And first of all, that the soul is not a mere tabula rasa, a naked and passive thing, which has no innate furniture or activity of its own, nor anything at all in it, but what was impressed upon it from without; *for if it were so, then there could not possibly be any such thing as moral good and evil, just and unjust;* forasmuch as these differences do not arise merely from

[2] *The Basic Works of Aristotle*, ed. Richard McKeon (New York: Random House, 1941), p. 880 (*Metaphysics*, 1072b). Emphasis supplied.
[3] Cudworth, *True Intellectual System*, 3 : 566.

outward objects, or from the impresses which they make upon us by sense, there being no such thing in them.[4]

He then proceeds to quote Hobbes with approval on the point that good and evil could not possibly come from the nature of external things, but he denies that the "anticipations of morality" could come from "certain rules or propositions, arbitrarily printed upon the soul." Their source must be, Cudworth argues, "some other more inward and vital principle" which "in intellectual beings" determines that they do some things and avoid others. This inward determination is a part of their essence, "which could not be, if they were mere naked passive things" (*ibid.*). Along with many others Cudworth felt very strongly that if the universe were admitted to be merely material bodies in motion there could be no ground for believing in God or in mortality, for matter, as such, would then be considered passive and spiritless and incapable of generating the "nobler" spiritual or religious values.

As for metaphysics, Cudworth, like Henry More, identifies it with theology. He offers a classification of speculative sciences which exalts "Theology or Metaphysics" as the "most honorable." The first speculative science, physiology, deals with things "both inseparable from matter and movable"; the second, mathematics, deals with "things immovable . . . but not really separable from matter"; and the third, theology or metaphysics, deals with things "immobile and separable from matter." [5] Metaphysics is understood to deal with that which is farthest removed from matter and at the same time most noble or worthy. In the context of seventeenth-century philosophical thought, that is, in terms of the Cartesian dualism of mind and matter, what cannot be derived

[4] *Ibid.*, 3 : 640–41. Emphasis supplied.
[5] *Ibid.*, 2 : 89–90. This classification is from Aristotle's *Metaphysics*, bk. 6, chap. 1, 1026a.

from matter is sought in the nature of mind. Hence, thinkers like Cudworth and More who were hostile to materialistic solutions to the problem of the interaction of mind and matter but were concerned with the status of moral and religious values naturally looked to the realm of mind for the source of these values. Cudworth's definition of theology or metaphysics as the most noble speculative science which deals with things immovable and separable from matter is consistent with the tendency to combine or associate problems of theology and epistemology under the name of "metaphysics." Henry More exemplifies this tendency by developing an epistemological argument based upon active innate ideas which purports to prove the existence of God. Cudworth employs the same kind of theory more directly and argues that moral and religious ideas must themselves have an innate source. Both men sought justification for moral and religious values by considering the source of our knowledge of them. The doctrine of innate ideas is most significant in the development of British empiricism since it points in the direction of the analysis of human understanding, the enterprise which engaged Locke, Berkeley, and Hume. That Locke opens his *Essay Concerning Human Understanding* with a polemic against innate ideas is adequate testimony to this point.

The Platonists were, broadly speaking, rationalistic as well as idealistic, and their thinking was in opposition to the popular experimentalism, which stressed sense observation as the chief method of natural philosophy. Thomas Sprat in his *History of the Royal Society of London* exemplifies the higher opinion accorded to observation and experiment as opposed to such rationalistic considerations as a concern for axioms. He remarks: "That this insisting altogether on establish'd *Axioms*, is not the most useful Way [to knowledge] is not only clear in such airy Conceptions, which they [the 'school-men'] manag'd; but also in those Things, which lie before every

Man's observation, which belong to the life and passions, and Manners of Men; which one would think, might be sooner reduc'd into standing Rules." [6] He is criticizing the "schoolmen" because they relied upon "general terms" and "Axioms" which had "no foundation in nature." He defends "experimental knowledge," gives Bacon credit for "opening the Orchard," and criticizes all who are "sometimes a little too forward to conclude upon *Axioms*, from what they have found out in one particular body." [7] This is the popular philosophy of seventeenth-century England: experimental natural philosophy which is supposed to derive the truths of nature directly from sense experience. As the success and popularity of experimental philosophy increased, there developed a corresponding impatience with rationalistic methods that stressed axioms, universal notions, or, in general, any kind of emphasis on the activity of mind as distinguished from sense perception. In this context the natural way to approach the problem of the nature of human understanding is to base one's theory on sense perception and play down the role of the activity of mind. John Locke does this and seeks to provide a theory of human understanding that is compatible with experimental natural philosophy.

Before turning to Locke, let us note one further approbative reference to innate ideas. It involves an attempt to use the innate-idea theory as a support for the axioms of rational thinking, a usage which appears to be quite independent of the dominant concern for moral or religious values. Isaac Barrow, Newton's predecessor in the chair of mathematics at Cambridge, interpreted metaphysics in an Aristotelian manner as the science of the most general principles. He conceives these principles to underlie all particular sciences and to be some-

---

[6] Thomas Sprat, *History of the Royal Society of London* (London, 1667), p. 17.

[7] *Ibid.*, pp. 36–39.

how innate or constitutive of the very nature of human reason. He calls metaphysics the science which "considers and defines the most general notions of things" and agrees with Aristotle that it is "the mistress of all the sciences." Barrow is concerned with the truth of geometrical axioms and is convinced that they must be demonstrated "by other axioms more simple, if any such there are, which are to be drawn from some higher and more universal science, as *Metaphysics* which is, or ought to be, the treasure of the most general and simple notions." He argues that no science demonstrates its own principles nor "makes any dispute about them, but takes them as self-evident." [8] Again referring to Aristotle, he asserts that the very meaning of a principle is that it is not capable of demonstration within its own science; but, he adds, "perhaps some of them both can and ought to be demonstrated without it" (p. 106).

As to how an axiom of a particular science can be demonstrated in metaphysics, Barrow suggests a kind of innate-idea theory not unlike that of More and Cudworth. Discussing the law of contradiction, he says that

> with respect to the origin, whatsoever it may be concerning others, this notion at least does seem to be immediately connate with our minds, and implanted in us by God, together with the faculty of reasoning to which it is intrinsically annexed. For there can be no reasoning without the admission of this principle. . . . This depends upon no other previous notion, supposition or argument, but is included in all reasonings, as the foundation upon which they are built. [P. 107]

Barrow is concerned with the problem of the ultimate justification of basic principles. Such justification he takes to be the task of metaphysics, and the character of that justification

[8] Isaac Barrow, *Mathematical Lectures* (London, 1734), p. 105. Subsequent quotations are from this edition.

is an appeal to universal notions which are innate and inseparably part of the very faculty of reasoning.

Barrow's attitude toward axioms is in contrast to that of Sprat. While Sprat scorns all appeal to axioms as antithetical to the new "science of nature," Barrow, a mathematician, takes a rationalistic line and endorses metaphysics as the science of the most general notions and axioms. Both men wrote during the same time, about 1655, and both were enthusiastic supporters of natural philosophy; but they exemplify two classic philosophical attitudes, empirical and rationalistic. Sprat, the empiricist, scorns reason as such and would make do with sense perception and rules formulated from it, while Barrow, the rationalist, would emphasize the architectonic function of reason and use universal notions to systematize the sciences. Sprat confidently assumes the validity of the senses, but Barrow finds it necessary to justify the data of the senses by means of a rational principle. Thus he includes in his list of basic propositions upon which "all argumentation depends" the statement that sense is "in its own way, an undoubted criterion of truth" (p. 108). As exemplified by More and Cudworth, the rationalistic attitude toward metaphysics is a sympathetic one. The empiricist attitude, however, is one of impatience, and the empiricists do not hesitate to develop their own special conceptions of the nature of metaphysics.

There was reason for experimental natural philosophy, or as it was often called, "the new science," to have a negative effect upon many persons concerned with religious and moral values. They associated the new science with materialism and feared that such doctrines undercut the authority of the Deity. Thus the metaphysics of the Cambridge Platonists was essentially conservative; it served as a prop against the growing popularity of the new science and also the materialistic ontology of Hobbes. But this metaphysics of innate universal notions failed to block for very long the popularity and influence of the new science, with its emphasis upon sense observation as the way to knowledge. The positive aspects of the new science became so attractive that most men of philosophical disposition ceased to worry about the supposed threat to religion and morality. Prominent natural philosophers like Boyle and Newton were very pious and found no conflict between the new science and established religion. Rather, they and their followers in the first half of the eighteenth century developed a theory of natural religion in which the discoveries of natural philosophy were specially valued because they provided impressive evidence of the divine character, the order, the beauty, and the harmony of the universe.

John Locke is a prominent example of a man with the philosophical attitude which combines approbation toward natural science and impatience with conservative rationalistic metaphysics. His polemic against innate ideas, in Book 1 of his *Essay Concerning Human Understanding*, affords at once the opportunity to examine the reasons for the decline of metaphysical theories based upon versions of the innate-idea doctrine and the emergence of empiricism as the dominant philosophical attitude. With the appearance of the *Essay* the possibility of any compromise between the new science and traditional religious values by means of a rationalistic innate-idea theory became remote. Locke's arguments against innate ideas were accepted by the great majority of thinking men. The basic reason for the success of his attack was that the idea of having two radically different sources of knowledge was thought somewhat repugnant. One of these sources would be the external material bodies in motion which cause ideas of sense (Hobbes), and the other would be the active spirit or mind which creates the universal notions which are the foundation of knowledge (the Platonists). Locke does not appear to belong in a clear-cut way to either camp. He seems to be unequivocally opposed to the view that mind or reason is an original source of knowledge, and therefore apparently belongs with those who consider matter the only source of knowledge; but, though he does adhere to a basic materialistic doctrine that particles in motion constitute the real nature of external things, he places no emphasis upon this issue. Locke is interested in the problem of the nature of human understanding, an epistemological problem, rather than in the ontological problem of what constitutes the real nature of things. This interest is a natural development of the conflict between materialists and mentalists (Hobbes and the Platonists) and the rise of the new science. The character of the new science, with its emphasis upon experimental sense observation, offers the possibility of a somewhat different solution than does either materialism or mentalism. Instead of considering only external bodies in motion as real, and the sensory experience or idea as a somehow less real "mere appearance," one could take the "mere appearance" as the more evident reality and reduce the external bodies in motion to the status of remote causes. This is the kind of solution Locke proposes and, broadly speaking, it emerges from a dissatisfaction with the dichotomy of matter and mind plus a strong positive attitude toward sense perception as a way of knowing.

In Locke's doctrine ideas mediate between the two supposed worlds of mind and matter since they are caused by external matter and are themselves the content of mind. The remaining content of mind, the "operations of mind" which manipulate ideas, has meaning only in relation to ideas. The ideas derive their reality or validity from their external cause, matter, while their actual character or nature is that of mind. This unification works only if one does not look too carefully at the relation between external matter and the ideas it is supposed to cause in the mind. In Locke's view the ideas of sense depend upon the real constitution of things, and in the case of primary qualities, the ideas also bear a relation of qualitative similarity since they represent the qualities in the external thing. Locke wants to be able to consider the idea as somehow containing the essence of external things, though, as his own analysis eventually brings out, he is not quite able to do this. He then has recourse to a practical attitude of regarding the idea as containing just as much of the essence of the object as we have any need for in the ordinary course of human life. Thus the dependence of idea upon external object, the qualitative similarity of the two with respect to some qualities, and the practical attitude to cover the deficiencies in this connection allow Locke to maintain that the idea of sense is a fully adequate source of knowledge. If he can show that there is no other source of knowledge, such as innate ideas, universal notions, or principles, then he has solved the problem of dualism since ideas adequately represent material things and are themselves the content of mind. Thus, though there is matter and there is mind, these only have meaning in relation to ideas, matter being their external cause and mind being a kind of apparatus for containing and manipulating them.

Turning to Locke's *Essay*, let us notice his definition of "idea." An idea stands for "whatsoever is the object of the understanding when a man thinks." That is, the term is used to express "whatever is meant by phantasm, notion, species, or whatever it is which the mind can be employed about in thinking." [9] Notice that he includes Hobbes's term "phantasm," the Platonists' term "notion," and the Aristotelian term "species." These terms, if not deliberately chosen, are particularly appropriate since they very nicely indicate the three competing theories of knowledge. They each denote the content of mind and connote an alternative theory concerning

[9] John Locke, *An Essay concerning Human Understanding*, Introduction, par. 8. Subsequent quotations will be given by book, chapter, and paragraph.

the origin of that content. "Phantasm" connotes the external material object as the source of the content, "notion" connotes mind, and "species" connotes the form which subsists identically or similarly in both mind and object. The source of the idea in each case refers to an ontological theory, while consideration of the idea itself and its relations to other ideas is epistemological. The term "idea" may connote a fourth logical possibility regarding the source of the idea, that is, independence from mind, matter, and form. The idea may then be regarded as the primitive datum of experience and knowledge. (Such a position was later developed by David Hume.)

Just as with Hobbes and the Platonists, a big issue with Locke is the source of ideas—where they come from. In his view they do not come originally from the mind itself because the mind is like "white paper, void of all characters." As to where the materials of reason and knowledge do come from: "To this I answer in one word, from experience; in that all our knowledge is founded, and from that it ultimately derives itself." This experience is resolved into "operations employed either about external sensible objects, or about the internal operations of our minds," and these two sources are "the fountains of knowledge from whence all the ideas we have or can naturally have do spring" (bk. 2, chap. 1, par. 2). There is, of course, a considerable difference between these two sources. Ideas originating in the internal operations of our minds, ideas of reflection, "could not be had from things without." They are just as distinct as the ideas we get from external things, although "this source of ideas every man has wholly in himself" (par. 4). The operations of the mind are assumed to function first about the ideas derived from sensation and then about "ideas of reflection." Though we have ideas as well as passions arising from the operations of the mind, there are not supposed to be any such operations at all unless there are first ideas of sense. Man begins to think "when he first has any sensation; for, since there appear not to be any ideas in the mind before the senses have conveyed any in, I conceive that ideas in the understanding are coeval with sensation" (par. 23). For Locke, then, the operations of mind are not to be regarded as having any significant independence of the ideas of sensation, and his intention of assigning the chief role in the process of human understanding to the ideas of sense is evident.

Regarding matter, or the real constitution of external things, Locke maintains that there are qualities in the external thing which correspond to the ideas of sense in the mind. We must distinguish ideas, he says, "as they are ideas or perceptions in our minds, and as they are modifications of matter in the bodies that cause such perceptions in us." The chief relation between the idea and the external modification of matter in the thing is causation and not similarity. "Most of those ideas of sensation being in the mind [are] no more the likeness of something without us than the names that stand for them are the likeness of our ideas" (chap. 8, par. 7). The exception to this dictum is, of course, the primary qualities which are "utterly inseparable from the body" and which mind finds in every "particle of matter," whether it can perceive it or not (par. 9). In other words, for the primary qualities (solidity, extension, figure, motion, and number) there is a relation of qualitative similarity between idea and thing in addition to the causal relation. Things in themselves have primary, secondary, and tertiary qualities, the secondary qualities consisting only in the power to produce the ideas of colors, sounds, smells, and the like in our minds, and the tertiary qualities consisting in the power to produce changes in other things. We get no clue concerning the nature of the real constitution of external things from the causal relation itself. Locke can only say that the objects have a power to cause ideas in us and admits that the senses do not give us a clear and distinct idea of this power. However, Locke is not concerned with the nature of external things but simply with their effect on the mind. He is willing to make whatever inferences appear necessary in respect to the nature of things, to the extent that they are the cause of ideas, but he is not interested in reducing ideas to anything like bodies in motion. If we had more acute faculties, he observes, we could

> perceive the severally modified extensions and motions of these minute bodies, which produce those several sensations in us. But my present purpose being only to inquire into the knowledge the mind has of things, by those ideas and appearances which God has fitted it to receive from them, and how the mind comes by that knowledge; rather than into their causes or manner of production, I shall not, contrary to the design of this *Essay*, set myself to inquire philosophically into the peculiar constitution of *bodies*, and the configuration of parts, whereby *they* have the power to produce in us the ideas of their sensible qualities. [Chap. 21, par. 75]

Locke is at cross-purposes with Hobbes. Hobbes regards the ideas of sense, his phantasms, as something less than real since they are mere appearances which are instrumental to a knowledge of causes (which are "real" in the fullest sense). Locke regards ideas as certainly real, and the external material bodies as causes that are remote and unknowable in their essence or real constitution. However, Locke's account is consistent with Hobbes's materialistic ontology, for he does suppose that the causes of ideas of sense are "motions of these minute bodies," though he is skeptical about the possibility of having any clear idea of their "substance." Locke wishes to leave the way open for believing in a materialistic ontology in conjunction with his own doctrine of ideas, and his treatment of primary qualities is evidence of this point. His attribution of qualitative similarity to primary qualities in things and their ideas in the mind may be either simply a concession to common sense or, perhaps, a failure to fully draw out the relativity arguments he admits in the case of secondary qualities. Either or both of these views may be correct, but it should also be noticed that the primary qualities are exactly those of material bodies in motion. Hobbes's atoms are solid, extended, numerous, and in motion; they are what constitute the real external world independent of mind. Just so, Locke's primary qualities are supposed to be inseparable from the object and to constitute its real nature, what it is apart from our senses or minds. Thus Locke's theory of primary qualities is a concession to the materialistic ontology that was presupposed in connection with experimental natural philosophy.

Locke's analysis of the idea of solidity offers further evidence of the intimate connection between the theory of primary qualities and the materialistic ontology. All the primary qualities except solidity are derived from at least two different senses; for example, we can derive the idea of extension from sight and from touch independently. It may be argued with plausibility that if we get an idea independently from two different senses and these senses are significantly different in character, then the idea may be supposed to have objective validity. What is common to the ideas of two different senses is what is supposed to be the real nature of the external thing, for example, motion, an idea derived from both sight and touch. This kind of justification may be used for all the primary qualities except solidity, but it may not be used for any of the secondary qualities. If an idea is derived from only one sense, sound, for example, there is a suspicion that it may derive its peculiar character from the nature of the sensory apparatus and bear no qualitative similarity to its cause in the external world. This is true for all supposed secondary qualities, and the idea of solidity falls into the same category, being derived from only the one sense of touch. Yet Locke calls it a primary quality. He does so, not merely as an adherence to common sense, but because he presupposed a materialistic ontology whereby minute solid bodies in motion constitute the nature of things in themselves. Speaking of solidity he remarks:

> Though our senses take no notice of it, but in masses of matter, of a sufficient bulk to cause a sensation in us; yet the mind, having once got this idea from such grosser sensible bodies, traces it further; and considers it, as well as figure, in the minutest particle of matter that can exist; and finds it inseparably inherent in body, wherever and however modified. [Chap. 4, par. 1]

Accepting this materialistic ontology, he further argues that it is founded upon or derived from the idea of solidity.[10] If he had no predisposition in favor of the materialistic ontology he would probably have realized (as Berkeley did) that solidity must have the same status as the ideas of sounds, colors, smells, and so on. Since these ideas are peculiar to one sense, he did not regard them as representing the real constitution of external things. He considered the idea of solidity an exception because of the intimate relation between it and the ontological conception of independent material bodies in motion.

Locke's ambition was to comprehend the materialistic ontology in his theory of ideas by laying heavy stress on the causal relation between external objects and ideas in the mind. The ideas themselves are of primary importance since they are experienced directly and clearly; external material bodies are significant as the causes of the ideas, but these are not experienced directly or known clearly. Though the ideas

---

[10] The same position with similar argument may be found in Newton's *Principia* (bk. 3, "Rules for Reasoning in Philosophy"). Newton utilizes the principle that the whole must result from the parts, so since the whole of a sensible body is solid then the parts also must be solid. The use of this argument indicates an uncritical acceptance of the materialistic ontology and is, I should think, an instance of the informal logical fallacy of division.

depend upon their causes, these causes are inaccessible to direct examination. As his analysis proceeds throughout the *Essay*, Locke mentions less and less the resemblance our ideas bear to the real constitution of things (in the case of primary qualities) and stresses the causal relation; in his distinction in Book 3 between nominal essence and real essence he comes very close to a position of complete skepticism with respect to the possibility of our knowing anything about the real nature of external things. He uses pragmatic arguments to blunt the force of this skepticism. What we know as a thing in terms of abstract ideas of species, or sorts, or classes is called the "nominal essence" in order "to distinguish it from the real constitution of substances, upon which depends this nominal essence" (bk. 3, chap. 6, par. 2). The real constitution of things is called the "real essence," and of this he remarks that we "know it not" since "our faculties carry us no further toward the knowledge and distinction of substances, than a collection of those sensible ideas which we observe in them." And, more clearly: "It is evident the internal constitution, whereon their properties depend, is unknown to us" (par. 9).

According to Locke, then, it would appear that we cannot get beyond our ideas, and his definition of knowledge as "nothing but the perception of the connection or agreement, or disagreement and repugnancy of any of our ideas" is consistent with this view (bk. 4, chap. 1, par. 2). But Locke continues with his ontological worry about the real constitution of things and says that "our knowledge therefore is real, only so far as there is a conformity between our ideas and the reality of things" (chap. 4, par. 3). With the sharp distinction he has drawn between nominal essence and real essence one wonders how there can be any conformity. The term "conformity" suggests a kind of similarity such as ideas of primary qualities are supposed to bear to their causes in external things, but even this similarity is impossible when the distinction between real essence and nominal essence is accepted. However, Locke now claims that all simple ideas agree with things, for they are "the natural and regular productions of things without us, really operating upon us, and so carry with them all the conformity which is intended, or which our state requires: for they represent things, under those appearances which they are fitted to produce in us" (par. 4). In this remarkable passage Locke attempts to repair all the damage of his previous skeptical remarks. He maintains that all simple ideas agree and conform to real external objects, and the terms "agree" and "conform" certainly suggest qualitative similarity. But he could not mean to imply this, because similarity is supposed to obtain only with respect to the primary qualities. When he says that ideas agree with things because they are the natural productions of external things it is the causal relation, and the causal relation alone, that he refers to by the terms "agree" and "conform." He uses these words to make the causal relation appear stronger so that it will come closer to doing the work of the relation of similarity. If this trick fails we must be satisfied with the pragmatic argument that, though our ideas are not so like things as we would wish, they nevertheless are adequate for the ordinary course of life. Regardless of whether our ideas are like external things, we have no choice but to accept them and use them since they are all we have for the pursuit of knowledge and for daily living.

Locke's general position, then, despite his many qualifications and candid admissions of troublesome details, is that as far as our knowledge goes, the basic reality is the idea. Its reality is derived from its causal relation to external things. He also regards external things as real but must admit, sometimes reluctantly and sometimes with alacrity, that they cannot be known in their real constitution. Thus the way is laid open for doubting the reality of external things. In short, ideas derive their reality from a source which is in itself unknowable. Generally speaking, a dichotomy of external and internal is assumed, with the external being the source of the reality of ideas. This view is like that of Hobbes but with an important difference. Hobbes would not say that the external is merely the source of the reality of ideas but, rather, that it is the reality and that the internal is only a manifestation of it. It is as if there had been between the thought of Hobbes and Locke a kind of ontological movement of the real from external bodies in motion to the ideas in the mind. Materialists are supposed to be satisfied with Locke's doctrine because the source of the idea, its cause from which it derives its reality, is the external material thing. Mentalists are supposed to be satisfied since the idea is real because it can be known with clearness and certainty.

Locke's general philosophical position was outlined before his treatment of innate ideas is dealt with in the hope that his unyielding opposition to the innate-idea theory will thus be easier to understand. That theory has been intimately associated with the conceptions of metaphysics developed by Hobbes and the Platonists, but it disappears from view in the years following the publication of Locke's *Essay*. In explicating the conceptions of metaphysics associated with the development of British empiricism, it is necessary to analyze Locke's arguments against innate ideas and to look for the emergence of a new conception of metaphysics in his thought. Locke was concerned with effecting a synthesis of and eliminating the opposing materialistic and mentalistic theories concerned with the source of knowledge and the nature of reality. His own doctrine is materialistic with respect to the source of ideas, so he had to eliminate the mentalistic theory that mind or spirit is the source of the reality of ideas. The Platonists maintained that active innate universal principles created by mind or spirit were the most significant factor for the production of human knowledge. Such notions, they argued, could not come from mere matter. Locke attempts to show how such universal notions, and all knowledge, can be derived from experience without the aid of any purely mental or spiritual ideas or principles. "It would be sufficient to convince unprejudiced readers," he remarks, "of the falseness of this supposition, innate ideas, if I could only show . . . how men, barely by the use of their natural faculties, may attain to all the knowledge they have, without the help of any innate impressions, and may arrive at certainty, without any such original notions or principles" (bk. 1, chap. 2, par. 1).

Locke is careful to say that his purpose is to show how men may attain knowledge without using innate principles. He believes that the best he can do is provide an alternative theory which is more congenial to the spirit of natural philosophy. His line of attack is to argue—correctly—that the fact of universal assent, if this exists, does not prove that a notion or principle is innate. He admits that the existence of some kind of innate principle is the obvious explanation for universal assent, but he presumes that some other explanation is possible. Abstraction or generalization from particular ideas of sense, he maintains, accounts for all supposed innate principles, but such abstraction or generalization does not produce universality. He objects strenuously to all supposed cases of universality, even resorting to the argument that idiots do not assent to the law of contradiction because they cannot understand it. Likewise, he points out that children do not have any of these presumed universal notions and that it takes considerable time and effort for them to comprehend such notions.

Most of these objections which are effective against a naïve theory of innate ideas are irrelevant to the theory developed by the Platonists. However, Locke has one argument that may be directed against the active, potentially present, innate-idea theory or any other kind of dispositional theory. He argues that "to say a notion is imprinted on the mind, and yet at the same time to say that the mind is ignorant of it, and never yet took notice of it, is to make this impression nothing" (par. 5). Locke considers ideas only from the point of view of their fixed character and regards capacities or faculties of the mind as merely expressing the fact that the mind can have ideas. The nature of such a faculty, its extent and limitations, considered in itself before a given idea or principle is present to the mind would be relevant to a discussion of the causes of the idea or principle. The faculty must at least be part of the causal process, but Locke does not allow even this modest point because he is committed to the position that the only cause of ideas of sense is external. The mind is supposed to be as passive as a white piece of paper. Locke's peculiar doctrine that external objects in the natural world have powers which produce the various ideas of sense in our minds is a consequence of his refusal to allow that the mind may have an active part in the causation of ideas of sense. Since all innate ideas are disallowed and there is no point in discussing capacities or faculties of the mind as such, he is then free to attribute the entire cause to external bodies. Hence he must posit a peculiar power which resides in the primary qualities or in the real constitution of external things and produces the idea of sense in our minds. Thus the mental apparatus required for the production of ideas of sense is oddly and unnaturally foisted upon the nature of things. In Book 2 of the *Essay*, when he is no longer concerned with the issue of innate ideas, Locke admits that the idea of this power is derived from the mind, from the mental activity of willing. This admission that the cause of ideas of sense, this active power in things, is like mental willing afforded Berkeley a strong weapon against Locke: Berkeley argued that such a mentalistic active power could not reside in passive inert matter.

The reason Locke cannot allow any kind of a priori structure or disposition to the mind, as has been said already, is that he either assumes or is convinced that in order for ideas of sense to be real, their original source must be external and natural. Further, it appears that the meaning of "real" for Locke is something like "that which exists externally and independently of human beings and their minds." And admission of a priori character to the mind, any innate ideas or principles derived independently of experience, would contaminate the reality of ideas of sense. Locke is perfectly willing to admit the existence of faculties of the mind and ideas of reflection as long as it is clear that these do not develop or occur before experience of ideas of sense. He has the idea that what comes first to the mind must be, somehow, the most crucial or important factor in knowledge, what determines its reality. Evidently he thinks that if he admitted some a priori mental factor it would be impossible to regard the ideas of sense as fundamental. Any compromise on this issue would undercut the dictum of empiricism that the sole and original source of knowledge is sense experience.

After the publication of Locke's *Essay* in 1690 the doctrine of innate ideas declined rapidly in popularity, and by the time Hume wrote his *Treatise*, approximately in 1739, that doctrine was "almost universally rejected in the learned world" as having been "refuted." [11] It had been closely associated with the conceptions of metaphysics developed by the Platonists and others, and metaphysics, as a legitimate science, also seems to disappear from the line of thought we are calling "British empiricism." The attention of the learned world centered, aside from natural philosophy and religion, around the problem of the nature of human understanding and the theory of knowledge. Though this kind of problem is not

[11] David Hume, *A Treatise of Human Nature*, ed. L. A. Selby-Bigge (Oxford: Clarendon Press, 1888), p. 158. (bk. 1, pt. 3, sec. 14).

usually identified with metaphysics, there is a continuity of development between it and previous conceptions of metaphysics. Something like a metamorphosis occurs, whereby a philosophical concern with the nature of reality (ontology) is transformed into a concern for the nature of human understanding and knowledge (epistemology). What started as an ontological debate between Hobbes and the Platonists (materialism versus mentalism) develops into an epistemological debate when the Platonists defend their ontology by arguing that it yields a superior theory of knowledge. Thus, Locke, accepting the reality of matter, continues the debate in the next generation by attacking that theory of knowledge and proposing an alternative. Locke's general philosophical position has been outlined at some length in this chapter in order to bring out what may be called his metaphysical or ontological reasons for rejecting the innate-idea theory. Though he offers many arguments against innate ideas themselves, some good and many rather shallow, he has deeper, if less articulate, reasons for rejecting the doctrine of innate ideas. He feels that what is independent of mind is real, that is, external material things, and that the source of ideas of sense must be in the real constitution of external things and not in internal innate ideas. This kind of speculation is ontological in character, but as Locke proceeds with his analysis in the *Essay*, ontological concern is transferred to the epistemological problems.

The idea of sense, supposedly the basic datum of epistemological analysis, becomes charged with ontological character, so to speak, in the course of Locke's analysis. Finally convinced that the real constitution of external things is unknowable, he recommends that we be satisfied with our ideas of sense, for they are all we can know with certainty about external things and all we need to know for the purposes of ordinary life. Being satisfied with our ideas of sense means accepting them as real because their source is real even if it cannot be known in its inner nature. The idea of sense then, in this interpretation, is at once an ontological entity, so to speak, as well as the basic datum of epistemological analysis. This ontological character of the idea of sense, implicit in Locke's thought, becomes explicit in the thought of Berkeley, who develops a full-fledged metaphysics based upon the idea of sense.

Locke's rejection of the innate-idea doctrine was somewhat unfortunate, for it threw his successors in this line of thought, Berkeley and Hume, off the right track. If Locke had not been so adamant about innate ideas, the suggestions of More and Cudworth regarding the active role played by the mind in the process of sensation could have been developed in eighteenth-century Britain. As it turned out, however, this development was to wait for Immanuel Kant.

CHAPTER 5

Metaphysics as the Doctrine of Signs

Determining John Locke's conception of metaphysics and whether it differs significantly from those of his predecessors and contemporaries is not the straightforward task one might suppose. On the rare occasions when Locke mentions the subject, his remarks are almost always disparaging. Speaking so of metaphysics was not unusual since a strong antimetaphysical attitude prevailed among his contemporaries. During the last quarter of the seventeenth century and throughout the eighteenth century the word "metaphysics" acquired a meaning almost synonymous with terms like "abstruse knowledge" or "useless knowledge" and was commonly used as a catchall label for almost any kind of discredited subject or discipline.

Generally speaking, the chief reason for the prevalence of this usage was the parallel development of Newtonian natural philosophy, which acquired such enormous prestige during this period that other disciplines or ways of knowing that could be interpreted as competing with it greatly suffered by comparison. Hence when a philosopher wished to develop his own conception of metaphysics he usually thought it advisable to provide an alternate name for the subject, in order to avoid the negative emotive connotation of the term "metaphysics."

Thomas Hobbes did this, calling his own conception *philosophia prima*. Hobbes, however, wrote a generation or so before Newton, when metaphysics was still fairly respectable. Therefore his *philosophia prima* is easily recognized as a substitute for "metaphysics." When Locke wrote the *Essay*, however, the antimetaphysical attitude was already strong, so we should not be surprised if his alternate name for metaphysics—his name for a study conceived by him as a right or proper substitute for traditional metaphysics—is not easy to recognize.

All Locke's employments of the term "metaphysics" in the *Essay* are disparaging, though in one case, which we shall discuss below, he does use the adjective "metaphysical" non-pejoratively. He speaks of metaphysics as illustrating the kind of reasoning he strongly opposes, that is, reasoning from maxims or principles supposedly self-evident or indisputable. Correct thinking, he argues, must depend upon having clear and distinct ideas in mind, words being meaningless unless they stand for such ideas. Thus, he says, "the first and most palpable abuse [of words] is, the using of words without clear and distinct ideas; or, which is worse, signs without anything signified." Most such words have been introduced by the "several sects of philosophy and religion" to support "some strange opinions" or to "cover some weakness of their hypothesis." Locke does not think that he needs to "heap up instances" but recommends that his readers go to "the great mint-masters of this kind of terms" for examples. These are the "Schoolmen and Metaphysicians." [1]

Another kind of defective thinking that Locke associates with metaphysics is the use of what he calls "trifling propositions." These are propositions which are "certainly true but yet add nothing to our understanding"; they are "very clear and coherent discourses, that amount yet to nothing."

[1] Locke, *Essay*, bk. 3, chap. 10, par. 2.

It is plain, he says, "that names of substantial beings, as well as others, as far as they have relative significations affixed to them, may with great truth, be joined negatively and affirmatively in propositions, as their relative definitions make them fit to be so joined." By "relative significations" he means accepted definitions which do not correspond to ideas of primary or secondary qualities of things. "Propositions consisting of such terms, may, with the same clearness, be deduced one from another, as those that convey the most real truths; and all this without any knowledge of the nature or reality of things existing without us." By this method, he concludes, we may make undoubted propositions in words and not advance one bit in the knowledge of the truth of things. An infinite number of propositions of this kind may be found in "books of metaphysics, school divinity, and some sort of natural philosophy." [2]

There are quite a few similar references to metaphysics throughout the *Essay*, but the two offered above suffice to indicate that Locke holds metaphysics in disrepute and that he associates metaphysics with names or words and their use. The significance of this second point will emerge later in our analysis. It may be helpful now, however, to notice some examples of this antimetaphysical attitude in the work of other seventeenth- and eighteenth-century philosophical writers.

Anthony Ashley Cooper, third Earl of Shaftesbury, who was a pupil and later a patron of Locke, criticized metaphysics from an ethical or practical point of view. "As for metaphysics," he says, "I shall willingly allow it to pass for *philosophy*, when by any real effects it is proved capable to refine our Spirits, improve our understandings, or mend our manners." But, he continues, "if the defining of *material* and *immaterial substances* . . . is recommended to us, as the right manner of

[2] *Ibid.*, bk. 4, chap. 8, par. 9.

proceeding in the discovery of our natures, I shall be apt to suspect such a story, as the more delusive and infactuating, on account of its magnificent pretensions." Metaphysics is represented here as pretentious and useless because it promises much and delivers nothing useful. What Shaftesbury values is self-knowledge, and to this end he finds natural philosophy almost as deficient as metaphysics. "One would expect," he says, "of these physiologists . . . that being so exalted in their understandings and enriched with science above other men, they would be as much above 'em in their passions and sentiments." [3] But,

> if their pretended knowledge of the machine of this world, and of their own *frame* is able to produce nothing beneficial either to the one or to the other; I know not to what purpose such a philosophy can serve, except only to shut the door against better knowledge, and introduce impertinence and conceit with the best countenance of Authority. [P. 291]

He then claims that it is hardly possible for a student of "natural philosophy" not to imagine himself more wise and knowing than the rest of mankind, but says that such a person "is mistaken in his calculation" (p. 292). In general, Shaftesbury's remarks indicate a widespread respect for natural philosophy.

Isaac Newton, of course, was the great natural philosopher of the time, and the high regard accorded him can hardly be exaggerated. In the writings of John Keill, Colin Maclaurin, W. J. 'sGravesande, and others, Newton's name is frequently mentioned with adjectives like "incomparable" or "extraordinary." Locke, too, speaks of Newton and "his never enough to be admired book," contrasting its demonstrations

[3] Earl of Shaftesbury, *Characteristics of Men, Manners, Opinions, Times*, 3 vols. (Birmingham, 1773), 1:289–90. Subsequent quotations are from this edition.

with the supposed knowledge revealed by general maxims (one of the kinds of knowledge he calls "metaphysical").[4]

Shaftesbury alludes to metaphysics as the "defining of *material* and *immaterial substances*" or, at least, he takes this distinction to be a good example of metaphysical thinking. In relation to a distinction between mind and matter the study of material substances would commonly be identified with natural philosophy, and the study of immaterial substances would be associated with metaphysics.[5] Insofar as Newtonian natural philosophy may be considered a science of the material substance, its great success naturally led to a disparagement of metaphysics.[6] Metaphysics as a science of the immaterial substance and a kind of opposite of the science of the material substance was almost bound to be scorned in direct proportion as natural philosophy was praised. Compared to the knowledge of the material world credited to Newtonian natural philosophy, what passed for knowledge of the immaterial world was unimpressive to those who were inspired by that philosophy.

A good example of the scorn directed at metaphysics comes from a popular eighteenth-century account of Newton's

[4] *Essay*, bk. 4, chap. 7, par. 11.

[5] Henry More, for example, uses this distinction. See the preface to his *Antidote against Atheism*.

[6] It should be remarked that Newton and his adherents were more concerned with defining natural philosophy in terms of mathematical notions and sensory qualities of things than as a science of material substance. As Edward W. Strong remarks, "Sense observation, experiment, and sensible measures are held requisite, by Newton, for knowledge of properties of bodies and for formulation of physical laws" ("Newtonian Explications of Natural Philosophy," *Journal of the History of Ideas* 17 [1957]: 52). Newton was careful to distinguish between a mathematical notion of forces, which he sought to provide, and physical "causes and seats," which he declined to consider. Speaking broadly, however, there does not seem to be any doubt that Newton and the men using his methods believed that their natural philosophy yielded knowledge of the material world.

theories. This book went through many editions and was widely read in England in the second quarter of the century.

> We continually act (especially with regard to metaphysics) as Columbus would have done, if he had pretended to write us a complete description of *America,* and given an account of its inhabitants, rivers, and mountains, when he had only seen a little tract of this country, and did not know whether it was an island or a continent. We reason upon the *chimeras* of our own fancy; we destroy and build systems; we rain doubts, and think to solve them without agreeing upon so much as their first ideas.[7]

The writer offers satire to make the same point, comparing metaphysicians, or "metaphysical jockeys" to

> fine riders in a manage, who show their address and dexterity by making their horse go backward or sideways, and all ways, and at length, after having laboured round and round for two or three hours, dismount just where they got up. [*Ibid.*]

This characterization illustrates a widespread antimetaphysical attitude which was still prevalent two or three generations after the publication of the *Essay.* Although it is extremely difficult to find a writer after the middle of the eighteenth century who dared to say anything mildly favorable about the subject without elaborately apologizing beforehand, there were some defenders of traditional metaphysics. One of the ablest of these was John Sergeant, who wrote a long and detailed criticism of Locke's *Essay.* He attacks Locke from the standpoint of Aristotelian metaphysics, maintaining that knowledge must consist of "the very thing itself existing in the understanding" and not merely some copy or idea bearing only a causal relation to the external thing. He maintains that Locke and Descartes are guilty of placing the conception of the idea between the real object and the mind. The idea is nothing real and these "ideists" were forced,

[7] Francesco Algarotti, *Sir Isaac Newton's Theory of Light and Colors,* 2 vols. (London, 1742), 1 : 89–90.

thro' their want of Higher Principles, to build all knowledge, not upon the *things themselves* in their knowing power, but upon the ideas or *similitudes* of them; tho' neither of them set themselves to make out or demonstrate how we could possibly have our *notions*, or *first notices* of the things by them.[8]

Along with this defense of the traditional epistemological position, Sergeant maintains a firm belief in what he calls "metaphysics." He is "apprehensive" that Locke has become prejudiced against metaphysics, and for this reason Sergeant offers a summary of its "objects." First, its "proper object is those notions of things which abstract from *matter* and motion, and concern Being only." He would like to "display fully the excellency of that most *Solid*, most *Clear*, and most *incomparable science*" but he can only "touch upon" it at present (p. 114). His list of the things included in metaphysics is quite long, but the principal ones are: the formal or essential parts of physical bodies in common and in species, the essential unity and distinction of them, the soul and its proper action, the mind (which is part of the soul), its progress toward its last end, the notion of existence, demonstration of God, his nature, the existence of pure spiritual beings (with no matter or potentiality), and the distinction of numbers. Finally, metaphysics treats of

all these high subjects . . . with more close, more necessary, and more immediate connection than the mathematics can pretend to do; since the evidence and certainty of the principles of that science (as also of logic) do depend on, are subordinate to, and are borrowed from the Principles of the *other;* which is the sovereign and mistress of all other sciences whatever. [P. 116]

With this example of some of the extravagant claims made

[8] John Sergeant, *Solid Philosophy Asserted against the Fancies of the Ideists* (London, 1697), pp. 4–5. Subsequent quotations are from this edition.

for metaphysics before us we are in a better position to understand what Locke and the admirers of natural philosophy were against. The great "objects of metaphysics" which Sergeant extols are, for Locke, so many "mere words" which advance "not one jot in the knowledge of the truth of things." According to Locke the only way to such knowledge is through clear ideas, clearness being derived from the reduction of complex ideas to their simple components, ideas of primary and secondary qualities. If this attempted reduction of metaphysical statements to clear, simple ideas fails, then, Locke concludes, they are meaningless. The words used are not signs of anything, and, hence, these words are abused. Some metaphysical statements, indeed, are not completely meaningless, but they are trivial; that is, they are deductions from one another according to their relative definitions and do not reach beyond the words or definitions themselves.

For a traditional metaphysician like Sergeant, the relation between external objects and the knowledge of them in the mind is identity; the notion in the mind is the very thing itself, its form. For Locke, however, the idea in the mind is not necessarily like or qualitatively similar to its external referent. Though he does not always seem to have made up his mind about the issue, he shows a preference for the theory that the relation between the two with respect to quality is nominality. His terms "nominal essence" and "real essence" indicate this; the nominal essence, though depending upon and caused by the real essence, is unlike it in character, being merely a sign or name. The actual character of the nominal essence is determined by the nature of the understanding or the imagination; it is an abstract idea whose character is irrelevant, the significant thing being that it stands for or nonqualitatively represents its external cause. The nature of the external cause, the internal constitution of bodies (their real essence), is unknown and probably unknowable, as far as Locke is concerned. All that is necessary for life and science, he feels, is that the external bodies affect us in certain consistent ways. That is, they cause us to have sense ideas which we can know with certainty or agreement, ideas that are real or objective because they have an external cause which is independently existent in nature.

Locke objects to traditional metaphysics because it is based upon the doctrine that the mind is capable of knowledge of external things as they really exist. He considers such knowledge to be impossible and believes that we ought to be satisfied with ideas, which are all that "our state allows." He falls short of ridding himself of traditional metaphysics, however, when he ascribes qualitative similarity to the primary qualities of things and the ideas of them in the mind. Accepting the materialistic ontology of Hobbes, he thought that he must exempt the qualities of bodies in motion from the general dictum of mechanistic epistemology that the ideas of sensible qualities are caused by the external material bodies but are not like them in character. Asserting that some ideas are qualitatively similar to their external causes constitutes an acceptance of the traditional formistic epistemological position whereby a relation of identity or qualitative similarity is postulated between the idea in mind and the quality in the external object. This compromise position is not Locke's last word, however. The primary-secondary quality distinction discussed in Book 2 of the *Essay* is hardly mentioned in Books 3 and 4, where he develops the nominal-real essence distinction. His conclusion is that "our faculties are not fitted to penetrate into the internal fabric and real essences of bodies." [9] Though he had earlier in the *Essay* expressed admiration for Newton's work, he now remarks that he suspects "that *natural philosophy is not capable of being made a science*." By "science" he means

[9] *Essay*, bk. 4, chap. 12, par. 11.

a discipline where certainty is possible and which is relevant to human needs. Thus he recommends that we concern ourselves with "that sort of knowledge which is most suited to our natural capacities and carries in it our greatest interest" (par. 10). In short, "*Morality is the proper science and business of mankind in general*" (par. 11). We are advised to concern ourselves with our own behavior or "eternal life" rather than seek certain knowledge of the external world. This skeptical but practical position is the result of expunging epistemological theory of the traditional theory of forms. If there is no similar or identical form which is at once the essence of things in the external world and capable of being realized by the human mind, then certain knowledge of the external world is impossible. The model for certainty here seems to be the ability to recognize similarity or identity between a present image and a remembered one, as a person may be certain that he is in the same room he was in yesterday. Not only is it difficult to imagine the process whereby such a form could be realized in the mind, it is difficult or impossible to conceive of a proof that such a form is similar or identical to the essence or nature of an external thing. The form as the essence of an external thing is not available for comparison with the form as idea in the mind. The mechanistic theory, in comparison, sounds more or less reasonable to the modern ear, claiming modestly a complex causal process, with the idea in the mind as its product. However, the ideal of knowledge as what is like or identical to what is real in the external world is relinquished, the content of mind being only functionally or causally related to real things in the external world. In a sort of philosophical unhappiness over renouncing this traditional ideal of knowledge, Locke settles for a resigned but hopeful and practical skepticism.

We shall now try to explicate Locke's conception of a new science to take the place of metaphysics, about which, in concluding a discussion of real truth, which concerns "ideas agreeing to things," he finally suggests a positive meaning:

> Besides truth taken in the strict sense before mentioned, there are other sorts of truths; As, 1. Moral truth, which is speaking of things according to the persuasion of our own minds, though the proposition we speak agree not to the reality of things; 2. Metaphysical truth, which is nothing but the real existence of things, conformable to the ideas to which we have annexed their names. This though it seems to consist in the very being of things, yet, when considered a little nearly, will appear to include a tacit proposition, whereby the mind joins that particular thing to the idea it had before settled with the name to it. [Bk. 4, chap. 5, par. 11]

It is not easy to understand just what distinction Locke wishes to draw between real and metaphysical truth. In each case the core of meaning seems to consist in the correspondence between idea and thing: real truth is the idea agreeing with the thing, and metaphysical truth is the real existence of the thing conformable to the idea. Possibly the clue lies in the choice of different verbs, there being in this context a significant difference between "agreeing to" and "conformable to." Perhaps by "agreeing to" he means the qualitative similarity or identity of the formistic epistemology. This would limit real truth to the rather small category of simple primary ideas and their external referents, the primary qualities of things. Metaphysical truth, then, presumably would refer to the relation between the real essences or real constitution of things and the nominal essences or abstract ideas in the mind. This relation would be causal, but there would be no qualitative similarity. This interpretation is possible and plausible; further, it is consistent with the development of Locke's thought from the earlier position centered at the primary-secondary quality distinction to the later position centered at the real-nominal essence distinction. It may, however, be too broad and too simple; moreover, considering the later position regarding the relation between the external thing and the idea in the mind, it would imply that there is no real truth but only metaphysical truth. This sounds very unlike Locke at that time but seems not an unfair representation of his later stand. Regardless of our judgment of this interpretation we will do well to try another, one which, I believe, is quite fruitful.

The clue to this second interpretation is the clause, "to which we have annexed their names," which is part of the definition of metaphysical truth. Real truth is supposed to be grounded in the relation between thing and idea; metaphysical truth, on the other hand, is grounded in the relation between thing and idea which has names or words annexed to it. It is this reference to words or names that distinguishes real truth and metaphysical truth. Even in the earlier sections of the *Essay*, where mention of metaphysics was always disparaging, Locke usually associated it with words or signs. The errors of metaphysicians were species of abuse of words. With this earlier association in mind, we should not be surprised if Locke's metaphysical truth turns out to concern the proper way to use words or signs.

Alexander Campbell Fraser, who annotated the *Essay*, seems to miss this line of thought in Locke, and in his note to the passage under discussion he supposes that by "metaphysical truth" Locke simply means the true propositions about "ultimate" subjects like real existence, God, and the self (n. 1). This seems to be a safe, natural interpretation since these subjects have long been associated with metaphysics or included in it. However, when Locke discusses the issue of our knowledge of God he argues that the fact of God's existence is a certain truth and there is no hint that he means anything less than real truth. Locke does allow that we have knowledge of God by demonstration and not by intuition, but he makes it quite clear that he regards this as certain knowledge. He also claims that our knowledge of the real existence of external objects is certain, though we do not known their exact nature —we are certain that they exist. At no point in Locke's lengthy discussion of these ultimate subjects—God, the real existence of external objects, and the self—does he refer to them as known by metaphysical truth. Our knowledge of these three "existences" is supposed to be real, and Locke is well aware that to refer to this knowledge as "metaphysical" would detract from its legitimacy in the minds of his readers. Fraser's interpretation does not take into account the strong antimetaphysical attitude shared by Locke and many of his contemporaries.

When Locke speaks of "other sorts of truth," such as metaphysical and moral, he has in mind something more than a traditional division of subject matter. "Truth in the strict sense" is not simply about physical objects and sense perceptions, "moral truth" is not simply about good and bad conduct, and "metaphysical truth" is not simply about God, the self, and the real existence of things. This threefold division of truth is based on a theory of the relation between thing, idea, and word. Some indication of this theory is suggested by the titles of the divisions of the *Essay*, Book 2 being called "Of Ideas" and Book 3 "Of Words" (there is no "Of Things" since Locke declines to deal with natural philosophy). There has been no failure to notice the importance of ideas in Locke's philosophy, but the same cannot be said of words. This is largely Locke's own fault since he fails to develop his theory of signs, though he insists it is of great importance. He ends the *Essay* in what amounts to a plea for a new science called the "doctrine of signs," which, I shall argue, is intended to be a replacement for the defunct science of metaphysics.

Let us begin by examining how the thing-idea-word relationship clarifies the classification of truths. Truth in the strict sense, or real truth, concerns things and ideas. Moral truth concerns ideas but not things, being about our ideas with no necessary relation to the actual condition of things. Metaphysical truth, though it concerns things to an extent, is chiefly about words and ideas. In each kind of truth the idea is the core of the matter, the fundamental element. In one case the idea is related to the thing, in another to other ideas (chiefly those of other men in the area of human behavior), and in the third to the word. Turning to the division of the sciences, we find that there are three parallel classifications: the science of the "nature of things"; "that which men ought to do," or ethics; and—the doctrine of signs, "the ways and means whereby the knowledge of both the one and the other of these is attained and communicated" (bk. 4, chap. 21, par. 1).

The first science is

> the knowledge of things, as they are in their own proper beings, their constitution, properties, and operations; whereby I mean not only matter and body, but spirits also, which have their proper natures, constitutions, and operations, as well as bodies. This in a little more enlarged sense of the word, I call . . . *natural philosophy*. The end of this is bare speculative truth; and whatsoever can afford the mind of men any such, falls under this branch, whether it be God himself, angels, spirits, bodies; or any of their affections, as number, and figure, and etc. [Par. 2]

The title "natural philosophy" indicates that the external object in nature is the model for this category of things. The purpose of this science is to attain bare speculative truth, which is Locke's truth in the strict sense. The inclusion of God and spirits in this category is conclusive evidence that Locke did not intend his definition of metaphysical truth to be a mere grouping of traditional metaphysical subjects, as distinguished from physical objects; it is also an indication of the ascendency of natural philosophy as the model for human knowledge.

Locke explains the second science as

> the skill of right applying our own powers and actions, for the attainment of things good and useful. The most considerable

under this head is *ethics*, which is the seeking out of those rules and measures of human actions, which lead to happiness, and the means to practice them. The end of this is not bare specula-tion and the knowledge of truth; but right, and a conduct suit-able to it. [Par. 3]

Since this science is called "ethics," the appropriate kind of truth for it is what Locke has termed "moral truth." The science itself has nothing to do with the "knowledge of the truth," that is, truth in the strict sense, which involves a relation of idea and external thing. Moral truth means speak-ing of things "according to the persuasion of our own minds, though the proposition we speak agree not to the reality of things" (bk. 4, chap. 5, par. 11). Moral truth applies within the realm of ideas and has no necessary relation to the actual nature of external things. The ideas of right and wrong which men hold, their notion of what ought to be, are clearly dis-tinguished from what actually is the case in external nature. Convinced that we cannot know the real essence or real con-stitution of things, Locke had little confidence in natural philosophy. Ethics, on the other hand, he held to be the most significant science for human life and the one which we ought to pursue with the greatest hope of success. His opti-mism for ethics is based on its theoretical position in his classification of sciences as the one which operates within the sphere of ideas, thereby being exempt from the difficulties associated with the attempt to know the real constitution of external things. "Right, and the conduct suitable to it," Locke suggests, are more significant than "bare speculation."

The third science may be called the "doctrine of signs," with the understanding that the usual signs are words. (Or, he remarks, "it is aptly enough termed logic.") Its business is

to consider the nature of signs the mind makes use of for the understanding of things, or conveying its knowledge to others. For since the things the mind contemplates are none of them, besides itself, present to the understanding, it is necessary that something else, as a sign or representation of the thing it considers, should be present to it: and these are *Ideas*. And because the scene of ideas that makes one man's thoughts cannot be laid open to the immediate view of another, nor laid up anywhere but in the memory, a not very sure repository: therefore, to communicate our thoughts to one another, as well as to record them for our own use, signs of our ideas are also necessary: those which men have found most convenient, and therefore generally made use of, are *articulate sounds*. The consideration, then, of *ideas* and words as the great instruments of knowledge makes no despicable part of their contemplation who would take a view of human knowledge in the whole extent of it. And perhaps if they were distinctly weighed, and duly considered, they would afford us another sort of logic and critic, than what we have been hitherto acquainted with. [Par. 4]

The "other sort of logic and critic" is, I submit, the sort of traditional metaphysics defended by John Sergeant, and it should be clear that Locke intends his doctrine of signs to replace it. The reference to names and signs in the definition of metaphysical truth may now be understood as an intimation of this doctrine.

In his association of the relation between sign and idea with metaphysics, Locke has a precedent: Hobbes also denounced traditional metaphysics and wished to replace it with a new science. He specified that his "prime philosophy" was to deal with the "right limiting" of universal names of significations.[10] This idea is similar to Locke's doctrine of signs in that it is specifically concerned with the function of words and signs. Hobbes's prime philosophy, however, was actually intended to be a science which provided definitions of universal terms. Locke's doctrine of signs is much broader since it is concerned with the relation between idea and sign as such rather than with merely the signification of the sign. Hobbes's

[10] Hobbes, *Leaviathan*, chap. 46, p. 523.

prime philosophy, his interpretation of metaphysics, has the architectonic character of traditional metaphysics to the extent that it is supposed to be the foundation of the other sciences. This character is abandoned by Locke, who substitutes what may be called an "epistemological" classification of the sciences.

This classification is epistemological because it is based upon the special theory of the relations between thing, idea, and word. Natural philosophy concerns external things known through ideas; ethics concerns man's ideas of right and wrong, which bear no necessary connection to external things; and the doctrine of signs concerns words and their relation to ideas. If one begins with the theory that material bodies in motion cause the ideas of sense, one must face the fact that the ideas of sense are qualitatively dissimilar to their causes in the external world. This did not disturb Hobbes because his attention was upon the reality of the external cause. However, the successes of seventeenth-century experimental science, with its emphasis upon sense observation, change the focus of attention to the character of the ideas of sense themselves. At least this is what happens in Locke's thought. Simple ideas of sense become the model for certain knowledge, and the way is open to view the supposed real constitution of external things with either indifference or skepticism. For, since the supposed real constitution of the external thing is not sensed, its nature may not be certainly known.

This skepticism about the possibility of knowing the real constitution of external things is an indication of the decay of traditional metaphysics. The notion of a form or essence which is somehow capable of subsisting in the mind as well as existing in the thing is untenable in connection with this ontology of bodies in motion as the cause of ideas of sense. If the skeptical position with respect to the possibility of knowing the real constitution of external things is accepted, as it was by Locke, still the pressing question concerning the relation between thing and idea remains. If this relationship is not qualitative similarity, is there another one that may be postulated in its stead? In the physical and genetic context the relation between things and ideas is efficient causation: a series of bodies in motion impinge upon one another and eventually produce the idea in the mind. To the materialistic imagination this is a plausible theory in its concern for how the idea occurs in the mind, but the question of how the idea is cognitively related to the thing remains open. That is, in the intellectual context of identification and comparison there seem to be few, if any, similar qualities between the materialistic conception of things and the ideas of the mind. However, qualitative similarity is not the only relation that may be relevant and, taking his hint from the connection between word and idea, Locke suggests that the relation between idea and thing is the same type as that between idea and word. This relation is one of signification. He already has said that since the things the mind contemplates are not present to the understanding, it is necessary that something else should be present to it as a sign or representation of the thing—ideas. The reason Locke places so much emphasis upon the importance of signs is not merely that they are so necessary for communication and thinking, though this is reason enough. The point is that the sign is his model for the connection between thing and idea. The word as sign for idea is a familiar notion well developed by Hobbes, but the concept of the idea as sign for the thing is a new development in the line of thought with which we are concerned (though Ockham appears to have maintained a similar position).

Notice how signification exactly meets the requirements of the connection sought between thing and idea. It combines a recognition of a genetic or causal relation with a recognition of the absence of qualitative similarity. The word "book," which bears no qualitative similarity to the idea of a book, may produce, genetically or causally, the idea in the mind. The word is then said to be a sign for the idea. They are dissimilar qualitatively but the one gives rise to the other. Just so, the presence of an external thing is supposed to produce, genetically or causally, the idea of sense in the mind, which in turn may give rise to its sign, the appropriate name or word. Thus the idea of sense is the sign of the external thing, just as the name or word is the sign of the idea of sense. In each case a genetic or causal connection is implied without suggesting qualitative similarity. The external thing, the idea of sense, and the word or name are completely different kinds of entities tied together by the one relation of signification.

Locke hardly does more than mention this doctrine of signs at the very end of the *Essay*, and the signification theory explicated here is at best suggested or hinted at several times in Book 4. For the most part Locke intended the doctrine of signs to be a science of the nature of signs or a kind of logic rather than anything resembling traditional metaphysics. However, the application of the signification theory to the relation between ideas of sense and external things does involve ontological considerations. That is, signification between external thing and idea may be interpreted as an ontological relation. Locke, fairly clearly, hoped to avoid ontological issues, but Berkeley, following him in this line of thought, developed a full-fledged metaphysics based on an ontological interpretation of signification.

Before proceeding to Berkeley's application of the theory of signification, we will examine the beliefs of John Keill as representative of the views of natural philosophers in regard to this relationship between thinking, idea, and word. Like Locke, Keill, a lecturer in astronomy at Oxford and an ardent supporter of the philosophy of his friend Newton, had little patience with traditional metaphysics and rejected any attempt to discover "perfect definitions" which embody the essence of a thing. He recognized the necessity for definitions but added:

> It is not to be expected that these should be logical definitions, which consist of the *Genus* and *Difference;* or such as discover the intimate essence and ultimate cause of a thing defined; these matters I leave to be disputed by others; for ingenuously to confess my own ignorance, the intimate natures and causes of things are not known to me.[11]

With respect to the possibility of knowing the real constitution of things, Keill sounds very much like Locke: "intimate essence" or "ultimate cause," like Locke's "real constitution" or "real essence," is admitted to be a rather poor candidate for knowledge. What then did natural philosophers think they could know? They certainly were not skeptics. For natural philosophy, Keill argues, it is only necessary that the definition clearly and distinctly indicate some observable property. As an example he remarks that it is not necessary for the definition of "fluid" to embody the entire essence of fluid but only those properties that enter into its relation with other bodies and can be observed. Hence, fluid is a "body whose parts yield to the smallest force or impression, and by receding, are easily moved in respect to each other" (*ibid.,* p. 8). This definition suited the current experimental work, and for Keill and other natural philosophers, observable sensory qualities were the object of inquiry, what could be known with certainty. The "real essences" of traditional metaphysics are rejected for descriptive definitions in terms of ideas of sense. As Keill himself observes:

> And whatever acquaintance I have with bodies or their actions, I obtained it either by the help of my senses, or else deducted

---

[11] John Keill, *An Introduction to Natural Philosophy,* 4th ed. (London, 1745), pp. 7–8.

it from some of their properties, which properties were discovered by the same means. I shall, therefore, instead of such a
definition as the logicians are wont to give, exhibit a description;
whereby the thing described may be clearly and distinctly conceived, and likewise be distinguished from every thing else.
[*Ibid.*]

Keill finds it necessary to discuss only the two elements
word and "observable property." He does not explicitly distinguish between the external things, the idea of sense, and the
word, though it would seem permissible to identify "observable property" with Locke's idea of sense. Keill specifically
says that it is only the sense which enables him to have any
acquaintance with bodies. (But he also allows for deductions
from these sensory properties, and this could open up a new
category more rationalistic than empirical.) According to
Locke what we sense is the idea, and it is the cause of the idea
that is to be identified with the external thing in the natural
world. Keill regards what he senses to be the actual external
thing even though he readily admits he does not know its
"intimate essence" or real constitution. Locke regards what is
sensed to be, not the real thing itself, but an idea in the mind
which derives its reality from the fact that it is caused by the
real external thing. Natural philosophers like Keill were content to take sensory properties as basic subject matter without
analysis to determine how much of this subject matter is idea
(mind-caused) and how much is thing (externally caused).
Formerly, most philosophers had always assumed that the
object of knowledge was to know things as they really are, but
these passages from Keill indicate that the natural philosophers of Newton's age frankly accepted limitation in knowledge. The Newtonians generally were quite candid in admitting
their ignorance of areas of knowledge outside natural philosophy. They had confidence in their method, in its correctness
and its adequacy for solving all the problems of natural

philosophy. Along with this confidence was contempt, usually mild, for knowledge sought outside natural philosophy. This issue of the relation between thing and idea was of great interest to Locke but not to Keill and the other natural philosophers. As a philosophical problem it fell outside natural philosophy and could be scorned as metaphysics.

The growth of empiricism parallels the decay of traditional metaphysics. The emphasis upon sense observation in connection with the development of the new science gradually brings about the disrepute of rationalistic methods based on maxims, principles, or innate ideas. Locke's attempt to develop a theory of knowledge based on empiricism led to a kind of practical skepticism where knowledge of the real constitution of things was considered impossible and satisfaction with the senses was exhorted. The natural philosophers held a very similar view. They also scorned the traditional metaphysical goal of knowing the real nature of things and were strong empiricists. The difference in attitude between a man like Locke and a natural philosopher like Keill was that basically Locke favored the traditional goal of philosophy, knowledge of the real nature of things, and was unhappy with his practical skepticism, whereas Keill exalted the limitation of philosophical ambitions, and scorned the ambition to know the real natures of things. It is as if he, and natural philosophers like him, were perfectly confident that whatever is real or interesting or important in external things must be revealed in their sensible properties. The great advantage of this attitude is that it provides a standard, public sense observation, by which statements about things may be judged so that clarity and certainty in knowledge become possible. Any attempt to seek further knowledge in the direction of what is beyond the sensible properties is scorned as metaphysics. Since such knowledge is stipulated to be not from the senses, it is presumed to be merely a product of the mind. What is directly concerned with mind or its nature was called "metaphysics" or was associated with metaphysics in the middle and late seventeenth century and in the eighteenth century. However, metaphysics was regarded with increasing scorn as it was contrasted with the successful empirically oriented natural philosophy.

CHAPTER 6

A Metaphysics of Signification
and Active Will

GEORGE BERKELEY is the next major philosopher in the development of British empiricism after John Locke, and it is
in his work that many of the lines of thought we have traced
through his predecessors reach full development. The difference in both attitude and the kind of thinking involved between natural philosophy and metaphysics can be seen clearly
in Berkeley's philosophy. With respect to the possibility of
knowledge of the external world, the natural philosophers
were optimistic and confident. Regarding the possibility of
knowledge about the nature of mind and human understanding, they were indifferent or contemptuous. Conversely, men
like Locke were skeptical about the possibility of achieving
knowledge of the external world, believing such knowledge to
be beyond human understanding; and, while not exactly confident, they were very eager to inquire into the nature of
human understanding. The natural philosophers, for example,
John Keill, were content to regard what they sensed to be the
actual material, external world and they disdained any
"secret causes" supposed to lie beyond what they sensed. The

philosophers, men like Locke, Berkeley, and Hume, believed that what they sensed was, in varying degrees, mind-connected or mind-dependent. The most they could concede was that what is sensed, the sensory image or idea, is caused by either external material objects (Locke) or by a powerful, external mind (Berkeley), or comes from unknown causes (Hume). These men take the role of mind in the knowing process very seriously and dissent from the popular view that what is sensed is the external material world itself. This issue, explicit in Locke's work though not emphasized, is particularly evident, even conspicuous, in Berkeley's philosophy because he denies that the external world is material in nature and maintains not only that the idea (what is sensed) is mental but also that its cause is mental in character. This is the very opposite of the materialistic ontology which had been tacitly assumed by natural philosophers.

Aside from the general level of thinking involving a difference in attitude concerning whether the study of matter or the study of mind is the more significant, there is in Berkeley's work a development of the doctrine of signs suggested by Locke. This is a theory of signification and it is central to Berkeley's philosophy and is a logical development or continuation of the line of thought of Locke's *Essay*.

The discussion of abstract ideas in the introductory chapter of the *Treatise Concerning the Principles of Human Knowledge* will serve to introduce the theory of signification. Berkeley maintains that the belief in abstract ideas is the chief cause of our difficulties in the area of "metaphysical knowledge" and accordingly devotes his first chapter to an attack on this belief. He begins by denying that the human faculties are designed by nature only "for the support and comfort of life, and not to penetrate into the inward essence and constitution of things." [1]

---

[1] George Berkeley, *Treatise concerning the Principles of Human Knowledge*, Introduction, par. 2, in *Works*, ed. A. A. Luce and T. E. Jessop, vol. 2 (New York: T. Nelson, 1948). Subsequent quotations are from this edition.

Although he admits that man's mind is finite and thereby becomes confused when trying to consider infinite matters, he insists that the fault is, not with the faculties themselves, but with "the wrong use we make of them." If we have an appetite for metaphysical knowledge, he suggests, then God must have furnished us with the means of satisfying it. The difficulties that have "blocked up the way to knowledge" are "entirely owning to ourselves. . . . We have raised a dust and then complain we cannot see" (par. 3). The chief cause of these difficulties is the belief that

> the mind hath a power of framing *abstract ideas* or notions of things. . . . These are in a more especial manner thought to be the object of those sciences which go by the name of logic and metaphysics, and of all that which passes under the notion of the most abstracted and sublime learning, in all which one shall scarce find any question handled in such a manner as does not suppose their existence in the mind, and that it is well acquainted with them. [Par. 6]

The source of the trouble, Berkeley argues, is the mistaken notion that the mind has a power to form abstract ideas which go beyond particular sense images and yet are supposed to be true to the nature of external things. For example, we see objects extended and colored and, observing what is common to them all, frame the abstract ideas of color and extension. We then proceed to consider or think about color and extension entirely apart from particular objects. Or, to take a more concrete example, the mind, having observed that "Peter, James, and John, resemble each other, in certain common agreements of shape and other qualities," leaves out the details wherein they differ and forms an abstract idea of mankind (par. 9). Berkeley insists that he "cannot by any effort of thought conceive the abstract idea above described." He claims that he can abstract in the sense of imagining particular qualities separated from others but only if it is possible that they may actually exist separated from the others. Thus he can imagine a hand without a body, but he cannot imagine a hand without shape or color. So he denies that he can abstract from one another "those qualities which it is impossible should exist so separated; or that I can frame a general notion by abstracting from particulars in the manner aforesaid" (par. 10).

Berkeley is arguing against Locke, who held that most of our knowledge of things (if not all of it) is in the form of complex abstract ideas which constitute nominal essences. The mind is supposed to abstract common properties from the ideas of sense and produce an abstract general idea of that property. This theory is supported by common-sense introspection and is similar to scholastic epistemological theory, though Locke disregards the scholastic terminology. Innocuous as this theory seems, Berkeley is determined to discredit it and establish an alternative theory based on signification. He will allow only particular ideas which are particular images or sense impressions. The idea of a hand must have color and shape, that is, it must be a particular image. The problem of generality or universality is met by allowing general words: "a word becomes general by being made the *sign*, not of an abstract general idea but, of several particular ideas, any of which it indifferently suggests to the mind" (par. 11). This is the alternative theory which is supposed to eliminate all abstract general ideas and make do with particular ideas and general words. Our general word "mankind" signifies not an abstract general idea, but an indefinite number of particular ideas of particular men that one has known. Abstract general ideas are not merely surplus entities that need not be postulated, but they simply do not exist and to suppose that they do is to mistake what goes on in the mind. A good deal could be said in favor of the traditional theory of abstract general ideas as opposed to Berkeley's theory, but this is not to the point. We want to notice that Berkeley's alternative theory relies on a theory of signification, and we want to bring out his reasons for so strongly opposing the seemingly inoffensive doctrine of abstract ideas.

Looking to Berkeley's reasons for opposing the abstract-idea doctrine, we must bear in mind his deep concern with the role of religion and morality in society and his announced purpose of bringing about the "utter destruction" of atheism and skepticism.[2] Like Ralph Cudworth before him, Berkeley felt that the doctrine of materialism, the belief that only matter in motion was real in nature, was a threat to religion because it tended to make the Deity either unnecessary or at least extremely remote in the context of our understanding of the natural world. Thus Berkeley's ambition was to devise a philosophy which gave a prominent place to the Deity not only as a creator but as the immanent cause of human knowledge. To do this effectively, he had first to discredit materialism, and his attack on the doctrine of abstract ideas is directly related to the attack on materialism since abstract ideas are one of the chief means to knowledge of independent material things. He argues that there is no such thing as matter and that the belief in it is a philosophical mistake which stems from the belief that the mind has a power to form abstract ideas.

What Berkeley regarded as his most important discovery is that what is sensed is mind-connected or mind-conditioned. Ideas of sense occur in minds, as he often says, though to those who naturally presuppose materialism the preposition "in" usually suggests that something is physically located in the head. Things, which are collections of ideas, are where they appear to be but their characteristics are strictly relative to the nature of the perceiving mind. To suppose that things

<hr />

[2] George Berkeley, *Three Dialogues between Hylas and Philonous*, Preface, in *Works*, ed. A. A. Luce and T. E. Jessop, vol. 2 (New York: T. Nelson, 1948).

could exist independently of human perception and still have exactly the same characteristics they have when they are perceived he regards as absurd, repugnant, and contradictory. Analysis of this common-sense belief leads to skepticism about the nature of the external cause of our sense ideas.[3] But, Berkeley argues, skepticism can be avoided if the materialistic hypothesis is completely discarded and we stop thinking of things as having an unperceivable and unknowable material substratum which is somehow at the source of the actual perception.

With the two-world theory—a world of sense ideas and a world of the real external causes of these ideas—our knowledge of the external world is problematical and theoretical because our certain knowledge is limited to the world of sense perception. Assuming empiricism with sense observation as the model for certainty, the real world, that which is independent of human experience, can be known only by inference and abstraction. Thus Berkeley's strategy is to deny the legitimacy of the kind of abstraction that provides the rational justification for a belief in a material world independent of human experience. Though his arguments against this kind of abstraction have considerable force, he cannot hope to carry the issue without providing an alternative theory of general knowledge to replace the rejected abstract general ideas. Berkeley recognizes the necessity for generality in philosophical knowledge and provides for it by making a particular idea "represent or stand for all other particular ideas of the same sort."[4] There are no general ideas but only general terms; there are only particular ideas which are particular sense images—extreme nominalism and extreme empiricism (perhaps H. H. Price's term "Imagism" describes it best[5]). Particular

[3] See Locke's *Essay*, particularly bks. 3 and 4, for such an analysis.

[4] *Principles*, Introduction, par. 12.

[5] See his *Thinking and Experience* (London: Hutchinson's University Library, 1953).

ideas signify similar particular ideas, and only the word is general. No abstract general ideas of common properties are necessary since the sign serves the function of making inference beyond the particular idea possible. Only particular ideas are real, but general knowledge is possible since a particular idea signifies any member of a class of similar particular ideas.

The point that Berkeley does not emphasize in this theory is that it is the similarity of the particular ideas that is recognized and makes possible their collection in one class. It is by virtue of this similarity that they become signs for one another. Further, the similarity that each member of such a class of ideas bears to other members of that class is prior to the fact that they signify one another. Berkeley wishes to emphasize signification at the expense of similarity, but he is unable to get around the fact that generality is based upon recognition of similarity. He admits that the ideas signified by the general word must be of the same sort, and this means that there must be a similarity or resemblance among them. If there is some qualitative similarity among a group of ideas and if the mind is able to recognize it, then this recognition constitutes a kind of mental separation of this quality from the other qualities with which it is associated. But this mental separation is essentially the same kind of process as the abstracting of the traditional theory described by Locke where the mind frames general ideas of common properties. An idea of a common property is abstract because it is formed by a process of mental separation (being one of many qualities discernible in a thing), and it is general because it is recognized in many otherwise different things. Thus Berkeley's alternative theory of general ideas depends upon the recognition of qualitative similarity just as surely as the theory it is designed to replace.

If recognition of similarity among different things or ideas is necessary for Berkeley's theory of general ideas, then what is so wrong with saying that one can have an idea of that similar quality? If one, for example, knows what red is, he can pick out all the red objects in a large group of things and identify them as being red. According to Locke and the traditional theory, we know what red is and recognize it when we see it because we have an idea, both abstract and general, of red in mind. Thus we are able to examine a group of things, ignoring shape, texture, and other sensory qualities and considering only color succeed in selecting the red things. This paying attention only to color constitutes a kind of mental separation of one quality from many others, and the fact of such a mental separation or abstraction ought to be adequate grounds for maintaining that we have an idea of that quality. Such an idea would be abstract and general, though it need not necessarily be a sharp particular image. The fact of recognition would seem to necessitate an idea of the recognized quality, and yet Berkeley is committed to the position that such recognition either does not occur (which is false) or occurs without an idea of what is recognized (which is absurd or at least very difficult to understand). We are supposed to recognize similar things because they are signs for one another and not because we have an abstract general idea of the recognized quality. The contention that one can substitute indifferently one object for any other in the class of resembling things is supposed to make the theory of abstract general ideas unnecessary. However, such a contention would seem to be strongly countered by the reply that we may substitute indifferently because we recognize a similar quality. And the recognition of that quality is possible because we have an idea or notion of it, but not necessarily a particular image, in mind. Berkeley admits that there may be a natural similarity, and that the quality may be recognized, but denies that this is done by means of an abstract general idea. Recognition, according to Berkeley, is possible by virtue of a capacity or disposition of the mind which does not require an idea of what is recognized. This peculiar position is necessary because he insists that all ideas be particular. The recognized similar quality is not particular, for it is experienced as part of the perception of a particular thing. He argues that there can be no idea of the quality itself, pure and simple, because it does not exist in nature separated from other qualities, and, therefore, it cannot do so in mind. Persuasive as Berkeley's argument may be, natural qualitative similarity among sensory ideas and its recognition by the mind still seem to require a kind of abstraction that he is loath to admit.

As already noted, the reason for Berkeley's ineffective attack on the theory of abstract ideas was that these ideas make possible a way of rationally justifying a belief in the existence of an external material substance. We need to look more closely at the role that abstraction plays in arguments for the existence of an external material substance. Though the following argument is not explicitly discussed by Berkeley, I wish to show that his theory of vision and his doctrine of ideas are designed to counter it.

According to the traditional theory of abstract ideas, we see similar colors in many differently shaped and textured things and form an idea, an abstract general idea, of one color. Such a process can also occur when the idea or quality is one which is experienced by different senses. For example, we see the shape of a table and we can feel the shape of the table if we wish. The idea of its shape, then, is derived from two different senses, sight and touch. Now, suppose that it is pointed out that many of our sensory ideas are peculiar to one sense, such as smells—the fragrance of a flower is never tasted, seen, felt, or heard, it is only smelled. Since all smells are peculiar to the one sense, it is not unreasonable to suspect that their character may be due, in whole or in part, to the peculiar nature of the sensory apparatus or, more generally, the mind.

At the very least, the mind or the sensory apparatus is a necessary condition for the occurrence and specific qualities of smells. The question concerning exactly what exists externally and independently of the human mind and sensory apparatus then arises. Any idea or quality which is known by means of only one sense may reasonably be suspected of deriving its specific character, not from the external world, but from the character of the mind or sensory apparatus. Such ideas or qualities constitute a rather large class, the so-called secondary qualities of Locke (which were also claimed to be subjective by Descartes, Hobbes, Galileo—and Democritus). Those qualities which are known by two or more senses, then, are free of the suspicion of being entirely relative to the peculiar nature of a single sense and become candidates for the status of independent and external existence. Since we see things moving and feel things moving, and since seeing and touching are such entirely different experiences, then we have some rather convincing evidence that motion is a quality not dependent upon any one sense and, hence, is a quality of the real external world. Motion, as such, is not peculiar to any one sense, and since peculiarity to one sense was the ground for suspecting qualities of not existing independently, it is free of this suspicion. Similar analysis applies to most of the other so-called primary qualities, and the picture of the external physical world emerges as many differently shaped and variously sized objects capable of movement. (This analysis, however, does not apply to the primary quality of solidity, which is experienced through only one sense.)

Though this argument for an independent external world is hardly conclusive, it nevertheless has some weight. Berkeley, at least, was evidently impressed by it and went to considerable effort to refute it in his *Essay towards a New Theory of Vision*. After going through the same arguments he later uses in the introduction to the *Principles*, he considers the question,

"Whether the particular extensions, figures, and motions, perceived by sight be of the same kind, with the particular extensions, figures, and motions, perceived by touch?"[6] He immediately answers by laying down the following proposition: "*The extension, figures, and motions perceived by sight are specifically distinct from the ideas of touch, called by the same names, nor is there any such thing as one idea or kind of idea common to both senses*" (par. 127). He then supports this proposition with the argument that a blind man "would not at first reception of his sight think the things he saw were of the same nature with the objects of touch, nor had anything in common with them, but that they were a new set of ideas perceived in a new manner." He also argues that "there is no other immediate object of sight besides light and colours" (par. 128). And, "It is therefore a direct consequence that there is no idea common to both senses," because, obviously, color and light cannot be touched but must be seen (par. 129).

The apparent visual perception of the solid objects and the discernment of distance are accounted for, in Berkeley's view, by experience and learning, that is, by the correlation of our ideas of sight (light and colors) with the utterly different ideas of touch. We see, for example, a patch of colored light, and as we move toward it, it becomes larger, until we finally have ideas of touch, smell, and taste. After adequate repetition and instruction, we learn to give the visual, the tangible, the olfactory, and the gustatory idea the same name, for instance, "orange." This is not because we are dealing with one thing, Berkeley insists, but because these entirely different kinds of ideas are associated (they are in the same place, so to speak). "Visible figures," Berkeley maintains, "are the marks of tangible figures" (par. 140) and they "represent

[6] George Berkeley, *An Essay towards a New Theory of Vision*, par. 127, in *Works*, ed. A. A. Luce and T. E. Jessop, vol. 1 (New York: T. Nelson, 1964). Subsequent quotations are from this edition.

tangible figures, much after the same manner that written words do sounds" (par. 143). There is no more similarity, he argues, between tangible objects and visible objects than there is between an object and a word that signifies it. And, more generally expressed, he concludes that

> the proper objects of vision constitute a universal language of the Author of nature, whereby we are instructed how to regulate our actions, in order to attain those things that are necessary to the preservation and well-being of our bodies, as also to avoid whatever may be hurtful and destructive of them. [Par. 147]

There are, of course, many difficulties in this theory which need not be discussed here. It is necessary, however, that we realize that this theory will account for appearances in a general way, even though we may find the common-sense belief in one material object more plausible as the cause of the different ideas of sense. The notion of mutual signification of associated ideas replaces the notion of one substance. Berkeley's observation that we perceive only ideas and never the supposed material substance hardly shakes the common-sense conviction that there is one object experienced by different senses. Perhaps, however, it should be granted to Berkeley that this conviction is justified by some kind of inference— habitual, natural, and irresistible but, nevertheless, an inference. The purpose of his alternative theory of associated ideas which signify one another is to demonstrate that this unconscious inference is not strictly necessary—since another account will do the job.

In another phase of Berkeley's attack on materialism he argues that even if there is such an independent material substance it cannot cause our ideas of sense because it is supposed to be passive and inert. As such, it is incapable of activity and, therefore, incapable of causing anything since causing is certainly a kind of activity. This is a strange argument, but Berkeley relied on it heavily and it needs to be clarified. From a materialistic point of view, that of Hobbes for example, matter is eminently suited for the role of causal agent because bodies in motion are understood as the very model of causal agent. That is, motion and cause are pre-supposed to be the same thing, with matter being that which is in motion. But from an alternative metaphysical position (the "idealistic" or, better, the "mentalistic") the model for causal agent is the act of willing. When I lift my arm it is in motion, to be sure, but the cause is my willing to raise my arm; this is conscious intention, a mental activity. Hence, the mentalistic interpretation of cause is that since the willing precedes the physical motion, it is the willing not the motion which is the real cause or activity. Since matter is not supposed to possess the mental characteristic of being able to will, it follows that matter is passive and inert in the sense of being unable to actively cause anything.

Berkeley, of course, adopts the mentalistic interpretation, and one might suppose that the position that matter is passive and inert is a straw man he invented. This is not true, how-ever, for the proposition that matter is passive and inert was a tenet of Newtonian theism. Newton himself held that matter was dead, inert, and lifeless; and men like Richard Bentley and William Whiston expounded theologies including this belief.[7] Briefly, matter had to be passive and inert to lend force to the argument that God must exist as the active first cause or creator of the universe. Any emphasis upon an active or creative power in matter detracted from the force of the argu-ment that God must be the first cause or creator. Consequently, most theologians and natural philosophers of Berkeley's time were not only familiar with the doctrine that matter is passive and inert but accepted it. Further, the Newtonians, in

[7] See Robert H. Hurlbutt, *Hume, Newton, and the Design Argument* (Lincoln: University of Nebraska Press, 1965) for an excellent account of these theological positions.

opposition to Leibnitz, who maintained that force or activity was the essence of matter, were forced to emphasize the passive and inert character of matter.

Berkeley, along with most of his contemporaries, assumed that there is an external cause of the ideas of sense and that matter is passive and inert (if it exists) and therefore cannot be the cause of our ideas. Moreover, he presupposed—and sometimes also argued—that willing, activity, and cause are the same kind of thing. Matter, then, cannot be the cause of our ideas of sense; and with the further premise (the Cartesian presupposition of the era) that the external cause must be either matter or spirit (mind), it follows that the external cause of our ideas of sense is a spirit, or mind. Berkeley also argues that it is unnecessary to suppose an intermediary, matter, between the active cause (God) and the ideas of sense in the minds of man. Such a supposition involves a contradiction since matter is passive and therefore cannot be the cause of anything. Perhaps the obvious weak link in this argument is the premise that cause must be a species of active willing, but as implausible or far-fetched as this proposition is to the materialistic imagination, it must be accepted provisionally if one is to understand Berkeley. Allowing this mentalistic conception of cause, we can outline Berkeley's theory: mind A (God) produces (wills or causes) an idea of sense (the sensory image) in mind B (human perceiver). Of course we have no model for this kind of event in our ordinary experience, but we do have a model for causing or producing an idea in our own minds. We can, for example, recollect or imagine a sensory idea by an act of will—this is the true model for causing, according to Berkeley. Since these ideas of imagination or memory are qualitatively similar to the ideas of sense, they must, he argues (*Principles*, 25–33), have a similar cause. The cause of ideas of sense is, not in our own minds, but external to us and more powerful than mere human minds because ideas of sense are more vivid, enduring, and coherent than the ideas of human imagination. As to how this external powerful mind produces an idea in the human mind, we are offered the metaphor of language and signification.

Our primary concern is this use of signification that Berkeley makes in developing his metaphysical theory. Signification is a mentalistic relation, rather than a physical relation, in the sense that its model is the designation of a word to stand for an idea or thing—a conscious act of a human mind. Theoretically, the mind arbitrarily associates a convenient sound or series of sounds with some idea or thing so that the sound will stand for, or substitute for, the idea or thing. Thus signification is the basis for that communication between minds which is accomplished by a system of signs, a language. The metaphysical analogy that Berkeley offers is that the ideas of sense, what we see and feel as things, are like signs, or sentences, in a language which we understand. Sensory experience is supposed to be like understanding sentences in a familiar language. In ordinary conversation someone (some other mind) is trying to communicate with us by means of a common language. Just so, Berkeley maintains, the author of nature communicates with us, using a language, or system of signs (the ideas of touch, sight, sound, etc.). The universality among mankind of these natural signs is accounted for by the power and benevolence of the external mind, the author of nature. Different men experience similar ideas of sense in similar situations because the cause of these, the powerful external mind, is coherent and consistent. It is as if the author of nature were eternally making the same speech for the benefit of limited or finite minds. In human minds, signification is a theoretically arbitrary process; but for the author of nature, consistency and coherence are maintained because of the perfection and benevolence of this all-powerful spirit.

After understanding this outline of the broad metaphysical theory, we are in a position to look more closely at the nature of signification. In the *New Theory of Vision*, Berkeley makes only limited use of the signification theory, applying it to the relation between ideas of sight and tangible objects. The idea of sight is a sign that indicates a tangible object in some direction and at some distance. In this work Berkeley limits himself to the problem of vision and does not emphasize his identification of tangible objects with ideas of those objects. He treats them as terminal entities, that is, as real objects whose legitimacy is not questioned. In the later *Principles* and *Dialogues*, however, it is almost immediately evident that the five kinds of ideas which correspond to the five senses are theoretically equal in status. A large part of the first dialogue is devoted to arguments intended to prove that the sense of touch is just as relative as the other senses. If touch has the same status as the other senses and if the ideas of sight are signs for the ideas of touch, then the general application of the signification theory is strongly suggested. The ideas of touch, in their turn, may serve as signs for ideas of sight, or sound, and so forth. Any of the five kinds of ideas of sense may signify any of the other ideas of sense, this mutual signification constituting the "language of the Creator," as Berkeley calls it in the *New Theory of Vision*.

This general application of the theory of signification comes out explicitly in the *Principles*. In *Principle 65*, Berkeley says that "the *fire* which I see is not the cause of the pain I suffer upon my approaching it, but the mark that forewarns me of it." And, "in like manner, the noise that I hear is not the effect of this or that motion or collision of the ambient bodies, but the sign thereof." Thus signification takes the place of causation. If matter is not the cause, as Berkeley maintains, then he must provide an alternative explanation. This alternative, logical to the religious mind of the late seventeenth or early eighteenth century, is, of course, that there is an author of nature, or God. Berkeley goes further than this, however, and seeks to provide a theory of how the author of nature produces ideas in human minds. He maintains that this is done in a manner analogous to the way men use language. Thus he says in *Principle 66:*

"Hence it is evident, that those *things which, under the notion of a cause co-operating* or concurring *to the production of effects, are altogether inexplicable,* and run us into great absurdities, may be very naturally explained, and have a proper and obvious use assigned them, when they are considered only as marks or signs for our information. [*And it is the searching after, and endeavouring to understand those signs* (this language, if I may so call it) instituted by the author of nature, that ought to be the employment of the natural philosopher, and not the pretending to explain things by corporeal causes; which doctrine seems to have too much estranged the minds of men from that active principle, that supreme and wise spirit, 'in whom we live, move, and have our being.']"

The theory of signification has two levels or dimensions: one is the relation of the ideas of the different senses to one another, and the other is the relation of the idea of sense to its external cause. In the former (this might be called the "epistemological dimension") Berkeley argues very forcibly that there is no qualitative similarity among the different ideas. They are simply signs for one another and are associated in our experience; they often appear to be clustered in the same place at the same time. Likewise in the relation between an idea of sense and its external cause, the active principle or "author of nature" (this might be called the "ontological dimension"), there is not supposed to be any qualitative similarity. The cause of the idea is supposed to be an active spirit and, as such, must be completely different in character from the idea which it produces in the mind of man. This difference, as Berkeley frequently emphasizes, is that spirit or mind is an active principle and the ideas of sense are passive and inert.

But this complete disparateness of the idea and its external cause that the theory of signification requires is hardly compatible with Berkeley's repeated assurances that things exist in the mind of God when they are not perceived by other minds. As Philonous says toward the end of the third dialogue, "Do I not acknowledge a two fold state of things, the one ectypal or natural, the other archetypal and eternal?" The term "ectypal" suggests a reproduction or copy of a prototype or archetype in the mind of the author of nature. In this case the ectype, or idea perceived by the mind of man, is more than a mere sign since it presumably bears qualitative similarity to the original archetype in the mind of God. When Berkeley takes up this position, appearing to condone the belief that the idea of sense is a copy or poor reproduction of a real object existing eternally in the mind of God, he reverts to a representational theory of perception. The novelty and the force of his "*esse* is *percipi*" doctrine are that the doctrine is a presentational theory of perception. One could simply point out this inconsistency and observe that Berkeley's reversion to a representational theory was a response to critics who quote Scripture, and that it occurs principally in his later works. This may be an oversimplification, and even if it is not and Berkeley did change his mind, I should nevertheless argue that his true position is the presentational theory based on signification and active cause. He expounds it constantly in his major works and reverts to the representational theory only in the early stages of an argument or when hard-pressed by arguments based on Scripture which he is bound to respect. When he makes a concession to the representational theory, he usually accompanies it with qualifications which lead back to his true position. In *Principle 3*, for example, in speaking of the table he writes on, he says that when he is out of his study it exists, "meaning thereby that if I was in my study I might perceive it, or that some other spirit actually does perceive it." The second of these alternatives is the simple-minded theory for "the vulgar." The first alternative, the hypothetical interpretation, is consistent with the signification theory and might be reworded in this fashion: to say that a table exists in the study when nobody is perceiving it is to say that an active spirit exists (in the study and every place else also) who will produce in my mind the ideas of sense, which constitute the real table, when I enter the study. With respect to the archetypes or perfect copies of all ideas which are supposed to be in the mind of God, Berkeley maintains that they could be nothing like ours since to have sense ideas implies imperfection. Also, we could have no certain idea or notion concerning what is in the "eternal mind" anyway. Hence there need not be any qualitative similarity between the archetype in the mind of God and the ectype the author of nature causes us to have. Thus Berkeley's true theory, or serious theory, does not necessarily imply that there be qualitative similarity between our ideas of sense and their external cause.

Berkeley requires signification to do so much work that it is difficult to see how its supposedly simple character can be maintained. There appear to be at least three different kinds of signification: among ideas of the same sense, among ideas of different senses, and between ideas and their external cause, the author of nature. The first kind of signification, as when an idea of vision signifies another idea of vision, may be called "signification within categories." This is the case when the visual orange, the fruit that one may eat, signifies a woman's dress which is orange colored; the two objects "have the same color," as we would ordinarily say. Any one of a class of visual ideas may signify the whole class, ideas of the same kind. This signification is possible, and necessary, because the ideas are qualitatively similar, although Berkeley does not emphasize this. Thus, Berkeley maintains that we recognize resemblances among our ideas but he denies that we may have an idea of the resemblance itself. Such an idea would be abstract and general, whereas his position of extreme nominalism is that all ideas are particular (particular images). In signification between an idea of one sense and an idea of another sense, "signification across categories" I should call it, there is supposed to be absolutely no qualitative similarity. The orange we see is supposed to be utterly different in character from the orange we taste or smell; the one is merely the sign of the other. The association of the two ideas is theoretically arbitrary; that is, the red visual cherry and the round, smooth (tactile) cherry are ideas associated in nature, being contiguous in time and space, but we could easily imagine these ideas being separated. Their association is not really arbitrary because the author of nature presumably intended that they be associated in the human mind. The association is simply something given in nature which could theoretically be otherwise as far as the finite mind of man is concerned. Thus these two kinds of signification are different in character: in one there is qualitative similarity, and in the other there is no similarity, only contiguous association in apparent space and time. The difference between these two kinds of signification was either not noticed or, more likely, deliberately underemphasized by Berkeley.

A third kind of signification may be called "metaphysical" or "ontological," whereas the first two kinds are epistemological. While both signification within categories and signification across categories are relations among ideas, the relation between ideas in the human mind and the cause of these ideas, the author of nature, is one between ideas and active spirit as cause. Nothing like passive, inert ideas are supposed to exist in the mind of this perfectly active spirit. The mind of the author of nature is unavailable to human inspection and beyond our full comprehension, so the supposed archetypal character of ideas in the divine mind is a matter of speculation. On the premise that the divine mind is like human minds, Berkeley maintains that the principle characteristic of the divine mind is activity, which is like human willing. And in the metaphor of language, the objects in nature are the language of the author of nature, his way of communicating with other minds or spirits. Thus the relation between ideas of sense and their external cause is a combination of signification and active willing. We may describe the three relations (within categories, across categories, and the metaphysical relation between idea and its cause) as three kinds of signification, or, perhaps more cogently as combinations of signification with three quite different other relations —qualitative similarity, spatial and temporal association, and active willing.[8] Thus signification within categories is signification based upon qualitative similarity or resemblance: the orange dress signifies the orange in the fruit bowl because the two objects resemble one another with respect to color. Signification across or among categories is signification based upon customary association or contiguity in space: the visual idea of the red cherry signifies the idea of the round, smooth fruit because the two different ideas of vision and touch are associated in space, that is, they appear in the same place. Metaphysical or ontological signification is based upon the causal agency of a will or mind: the visual ideas of a sunset signify the intention of the author of nature that human minds experience beauty; or, a simpler example, the sight of fresh water signifies that if we perform the appropriate bodily actions we may quench our thirst.[9]

[8] Notice that these three relations correspond to David Hume's three principles of association—resemblance, contiguity, and causality. See his *Enquiry Concerning Human Understanding*, sec. 3.

[9] I omit Berkeley's account of mathematical and logical signs since this kind of signification does not bear directly upon his metaphysical theory. He holds that number is a mentally constituted sign and that as words signify ideas of sense or imagination (hence, things), numbers

This analysis shows that signification is not the simple relation that Berkeley proposes. It depends upon other relations, either qualitative similarity, association in space and time, or active will. Yet in his criticism of abstract ideas Berkeley attempts to substitute signification for qualitative similarity, failing to realize that the signification of his alternative theory of generality depends upon the recognition of qualitative similarity. His reason for seeking to discredit qualitative similarity is that it is the basis for the theory of abstraction used by Locke which makes possible some fairly strong arguments for the existence of an independent material substance. On a broader historical level this attempt to substitute signification for qualitative similarity is an effort to develop a new metaphysics completely free of the traditional formistic theory of Plato and Aristotle. Qualitative similarity is at the core of the formistic theory since it (or the stronger version of it, identity) is postulated as the relation between what exists externally and what is conceived in the mind as knowledge.

This attempt to get free of the formistic metaphysics has been one of the characteristic themes in the development of British empiricism. Perhaps a brief summary of the role of this issue will provide a context in which Berkeley's theory of signification and his metaphysics may be understood as part of a continuous-historical development. Bacon had little more than strong feeling and the intention to be free of the Aristotelian metaphysics. His conception of knowledge remained

---

signify the quantitative relations between things. His treatment of mathematical and logical signs is not novel except that he demands conceivability on a sense basis. As for a metaphysical interpretation of logical and mathematical notions, these may be understood as the manner in which the author of nature orders the ideas he presents to our minds. Metaphorically, since we understand the language of the author of nature, we are capable of understanding its rules of grammar and syntax as well.

essentially formistic. Hobbes, despite his development of a materialistic ontology, continued to use the Aristotelian logic and the formistic way of thinking in his epistemology. He failed to integrate the materialistic ontology with an essentially formistic epistemology. The Cambridge Platonists, Henry More and Ralph Cudworth, emphasized activity, as Berkeley did, and defended the formistic metaphysics in their attack on materialism. Locke made considerable progress toward the solution of Hobbes's problem, that of an adequate epistemology for the materialistic ontology, but did not fully succeed in exorcising the ghost of the formistic theory. The haunting remnant of this ghost is qualitative similarity which Locke still retained as the relation between primary qualities in things and the ideas of these qualities in the mind. His later position, developed in Books 3 and 4 of the *Essay*, constitutes one solution to the problem: denial of qualitative similarity between idea and the real constitution of external things. Locke appeared not to like this position very much, though he did suggest that signification is the operative relation between the external thing and the idea in the mind. Berkeley's metaphysics is a development of this suggestion from Locke.

Assuming a causal relationship between the real constitution of things and the ideas of sense in the mind, Locke further postulates the relation of signification between them— idea signifies thing (because thing causes the idea). This position suggests a general theory whereby the word signifies the idea and the idea signifies the external thing. Thus the three epistemological entities, so to speak, of word, idea, and thing are related by the one relation, signification. In the case of the relation between word and idea, signification has an arbitrary mentalistic character, as in the model of the stipulative definition where one designates a term to signify a thing (or idea). The relation between external cause and the idea suggests no such mentalistic or arbitrary character, though the relation is supposed to be signification. This latter kind of signification is akin to the natural sign of Ockham and Hobbes. In emphasizing that the one relation holds between thing, idea, and word, Locke tends to ignore the difference between the two kinds of signification, causal, or natural, and arbitrary, or mentalistic. Berkeley's metaphysics may be understood as an attempt to develop Locke's theory; that is, to exploit the notion that signification is the operative relation between idea and its external cause as well as between word and idea. He postulates one kind of signification, the mentalistic kind, in both cases; as human minds designate terms to stand for things (or ideas), the author of nature designates ideas of sense (things in nature) to stand for ideas he wishes to communicate to other minds. Thus the notion of active willing is integrated with the notion of signification in Berkeley's metaphysics. Signification is something a mind does; it wills that a sign stand for a thing or idea. Human minds do this when they stipulate definitions, and the author of nature does this when he communicates to other minds, using the language of nature, what we see, hear, and so on. The arbitrary nature of human signification differs from the ordered signification of the author of nature as the imperfect, fallible, limited mind differs from the perfect, omnipotent, all-good, infinite mind of God.

Now that some of the difficulties of Berkeley's metaphysics of signification have been clarified, I should like to look at some of his specific comments about metaphysics as a science. Unlike Hobbes and Locke, Berkeley makes few pejorative remarks about metaphysics, and when he discusses the poor reputation of this science he places the blame upon the "bad use" men make of their faculties. "We have raised a dust and then complain we cannot see," he remarks in the introduction to the *Principles*. At the end of *De Motu* he offers a classification of the sciences which gives some indication of his conception of metaphysics.

In physics sense and experience which reach only to apparent effects hold sway; in mechanics the abstract notions of mathematicians are admitted. In first philosophy or metaphysics we are concerned with incorporeal things, with causes, truth, and the existence of things.[10]

Physics treats the "series or succession of sensible things" and the laws by which they are connected, but, he adds, no account can be taken of the "actual seat of the forces or of the active powers" (par. 72). Only by meditation and reasoning can "truly active causes he rescued from the surrounding darkness and be to some extent known. To deal with them is the business of first philosophy or metaphysics" (par. 73). This emphasis upon the "truly active causes" is a reference to his own metaphysical doctrine, the active cause being the author of nature. As we should expect, then, Berkeley accords a legitimate status to the science of metaphysics and even sometimes criticizes mathematicians and natural philosophers for belittling it. In the *Analyst* he asks whether there is not "really a *philosophia prima*, a certain transcendental science superior to and more extensive than mathematics, which it might behove our modern analysts rather to learn than despise." [11]

Though this metaphysics of signification may be as fantastic to the modern reader as it was to most of Berkeley's contemporaries, it is interesting and instructive for a number of reasons. It emerges from a context of continuous epistemological inquiry through the better part of two centuries. Once the Aristotelian metaphysics of forms was rejected in favor of a materialistic ontology, the question of the nature and possibility of knowledge of the external world became

[10] George Berkeley, *De Motu*, par. 71, in *Works*, ed. A. A. Luce and T. E. Jessop, vol. 4 (New York: T. Nelson, 1948). Subsequent quotations are from this edition.

[11] Query 49, in *Works*, Luce and Jessop, vol. 4.

acute. Locke made a good effort to provide an epistemology compatible with materialism; Berkeley maintained that materialism had to be rejected before a consistent epistemology could be worked out. Assuming Berkeley's alternative mentalistic ontology to be unacceptable and his arguments against Locke's epistemological theories to be cogent, we are left with a negative result. The attempt to develop a theory of knowledge suitable to materialism and Newtonian natural philosophy appears to end in failure. The articulation of this result is to be found in the work of David Hume, though the outline of a pragmatic epistemology was already worked out by George Berkeley.

CHAPTER 7

Epistemology without Ontology

MOST OF THE CONCEPTIONS of metaphysics we have discussed
have either been directly concerned with or at least associated
with the problem of the relation between the idea in the mind
and the external cause of that idea. There have been materialistic theories of this connection (Hobbes), mentalistic
theories (Berkeley), and compromise dualistic theories (the
Platonists). There have been strong theories where this link is
central to a whole philosophy (Hobbes), and there have been
weak theories where this link is little more than assumed
(Locke). If a philosopher is concerned primarily with the character of the cause rather than with the idea or the nature of the
mind, he is ontologically oriented (Hobbes); a philosopher
concerned with the nature of ideas and the working of the
mind is epistemologically oriented (Locke). Characteristic of
the historical development of British empiricism is a gradual
shift of philosophical interest from ontology to epistemology,
or the study of human understanding and knowledge. All the
philosophers we have studied in the line of development of
British empiricism had some concern for the ontological problem of the nature of the cause of our sense ideas, even though,
in the case of Locke, for example, epistemological problems

predominated in their thought. However, in the work of David Hume, strong and persuasive arguments are offered which have the effect of severing this ontological thread, and bringing to a logical conclusion the line of thought we have been tracing.

In both the materialistic and the mentalistic theories, the idea is supposed to be caused by the external thing or agent. The conception of the nature of this cause is radically different in each case. The materialistic theory is based on the model of bodies in motion, while the mentalistic theory is based on the model of an active mind willing an idea or action. Berkeley offered many strong arguments, and some questionable ones, against the materialistic theory and provided an alternative mentalistic theory. Hume rejected Berkeley's positive theory of active will and signification but failed to reassert the materialistic theory. It is almost as if Hume found Berkeley's metaphysics so repugnant that he was led to reject the whole idea of there being an external cause or necessary source of the ideas of sense. Nevertheless he begins his discussion in the *Treatise of Human Nature* apparently accepting some kind of cause of perception, maintaining that the "impression of sensation" (Berkeley's idea of sense) "arises in the soul originally, from unknown causes."[1]

On further analysis, however, Hume does not admit that we know of any causal connection between perceptions and any kind of external independent thing or agent. Thus he argues that "as no beings are ever present to the mind but perceptions, it follows that we may observe a conjunction or a relation of cause and effect between different perceptions, but can never observe it between perceptions and objects" (bk. 1, pt. 4, sec. 2, p. 212). Since we cannot observe cause and effect

[1] Hume, *A Treatise of Human Nature* (Oxford: Clarendon Press, 1888), bk. 1, pt. 1, sec. 2, p. 7. Subsequent quotations are from this edition.

between perceptions and external objects, we cannot be certain that such a relation exists. We can be certain of our perceptions and relations between them, but the inference to an unperceivable external cause, either object or active willing agent, is either conjectural or meaningless. What was tacitly assumed by Hume's predecessors in this line of thought is now openly questioned.

Hume directly attacks Berkeley's conception of the nature of cause, denying that there is any such activity or active power in the mind. In addition to passive ideas, Berkeley maintains that we have knowledge of the self, which perceives and wills. This self is an "active principle" or spirit which we know by a kind of "active thinking image." Though this image is known as certainly as an idea, it is not an idea because it is not passive and is not about something passive; therefore he calls it a "notion." Notions are always concerned with the nature of mind or spirit or the activity of mind or spirit, and they are qualitatively different from ideas, which are passive. In Berkeley's theory the active willing of the author of nature is supposed to be the cause of our ideas of sense, and the active willing of this external spirit, or God, is supposed to be analogous to the willing of the human mind. Hume, however, argues that willing is just another passive perception; it is, he maintains, "nothing but the internal impression we feel and are conscious of, when we knowingly give rise to any new motion of our body, or new perception of our mind" (bk. 2, pt. 3, sec. 1, p. 399). The self which Berkeley knows intuitively Hume maintains is "nothing but a heap or collection of different perceptions, united together by certain relations." When he looks for the self he always stumbles on "some particular perception or other, of heat or cold, light or shade, love or hatred, pain or pleasure." Further, he says, "I never can catch *myself* at any time without a perception, and never can observe anything but the perception" (bk. 1, pt. 4, sec. 6, p. 252). According to Hume, then, there is no such thing as the active will or a self that wills and observes; there are only passive perceptions related in various ways.

Ontological metaphysics in the development of British empiricism comes to a dead end in these arguments of Hume (as far as they are accepted, of course). He cuts the last slender thread between the perceptions of the mind and any kind of independent external cause. This does not mean that anyone ceases to believe in external causes of perceptions or independent physical objects, for as he remarks, the imagination or fancy is so strong that he takes it for granted that "whatever may be the reader's opinion at this present moment, that an hour hence he will be persuaded there is both an external and internal world" (bk. 1, pt. 4, sec. 2, p. 218). It is the imagination or fancy and not reason or the senses that leads us to believe in this double world. Ontological metaphysics is concerned with establishing a rational theory of the link between these two supposed worlds, but Hume's arguments, if correct, establish that only imagination can possibly operate in this area. To the extent that metaphysics is based on reason there is the hope that it can achieve some degree of certainty and lay claim to being a rational discipline. But if metaphysics is dissociated from reason and must depend upon imagination it is open to the charge of being in the same class with wish-fulfillment dreams or idle conjecture, for which general agreement among men is unlikely. Reason cannot trust imagination and if the only way to knowledge of an independent external world is through imagination, then philosophers, as men of reason, ought to give up looking for such knowledge. Thus, no matter how strongly our imaginations assure us that there is an independent external world which is the source of our perceptions, "profound and intense reflection" leads us to a "skeptical doubt" that we must respect.

These views of Hume should be routinely familiar to the student of philosophy, and I outline them here only to show their bearing on Berkeley's metaphysics. From the standpoint of Hume's analysis of causation and activity there is no longer any place for ontological speculation. Berkeley's mentalistic conception of cause as active will is denied and the materialistic conception of cause is ignored. Causation as conceived by Hume's predecessors was a relation that penetrated beyond the level of ideas of sense to an external reality, but in Hume's analysis it is reduced to being a relation among perceptions. There are no solid rational grounds for believing in anything beyond the sphere of our perceptions—such is the general conclusion to which Hume comes.

With the force of his analysis of cause, self, and activity in mind it is at least somewhat surprising to find Hume defending "metaphysics." In *An Enquiry concerning Human Understanding* he draws a distinction between the "obvious philosophy of common sense" and the more "accurate and abstruse philosophy." The generality of mankind naturally prefers the easy philosophy but, he remarks, "as the matter is often carried farther, even to the absolute rejecting of all profound reasonings, or what is commonly called *metaphysics* we shall now proceed to consider what can reasonably be pleaded in their behalf." [2] The "justest and most plausible objection" to metaphysics, he says, is that much of it arises from "the fruitless efforts of human vanity, which would penetrate into subjects utterly inaccessible to the understanding." But this is no reason to abandon metaphysics, for to do so would be to give up to "blind despair." This motive "can never reasonably have place in the sciences; since, however unsuccessful former attempts may have proved, there is still room to hope, that the industry, good fortune, or improved sagacity of succeeding generations may reach discoveries unknown to former ages" (sec. 1, par. 7, p. 12).

[2] *An Enquiry concerning Human Understanding*, in *Hume's Enquiries* 2nd edition by L. A. Selby-Bigge (Oxford: Clarendon Press, 1966). Reprinted from the posthumous edition of 1777, sec. 1, paragraph 5, p. 9.

Hume wants to continue working with metaphysics and he speaks as if he had a definite idea of how to go about it. That way is "to inquire seriously into the nature of human understanding, and show, from exact analysis of its powers and capacity, that it is by no means fitted for such remote and abstruse subjects." We must "submit to this fatigue" and "cultivate true metaphysics" so that we may destroy "the false and the adulterate." By "true metaphysics" he means the inquiry into the nature of human understanding in order to discover the "proper province of human reason." It is "no inconsiderable part of science," he remarks, "barely to know the different operations of the mind, to separate them from each other, to class them under their proper heads, and to correct all seeming disorder." His hope is that "the secret springs and principles, by which the human mind is actuated in its operations" eventually will be discovered (par. 7–9, pp. 12–14).

This true metaphysics Hume speaks of is not exactly novel. Both Locke and Berkeley expressed similar goals, though they did not identify the study of human understanding with metaphysics as Hume did. Perhaps it can be said that they still had some traditional metaphysical ambition and hoped to find a way for human knowledge to reach to an external independent cause of our sense ideas. Locke started ambitiously and eventually reached a skepticism almost as deep as Hume's, though not as straightforward. Berkeley may be understood to have constructed a whole new metaphysics in order to avoid skepticism (and atheism). This association of skepticism with respect to the possibility of knowing the nature of an independent external world (or even that there is such a world) and the identification of metaphysics with the study of human understanding or human nature is the outcome of a continuous development of a line of thought that began with Hobbes. The congeniality of his materialistic ontology and the natural philosophy of the latter half of the seventeenth century made the whole notion of further speculation in ontology uninteresting. The focus of attention was definitely in the direction of natural philosophy, and natural philosophers were happy to assume that the external world was composed of material bodies in motion and proceed to more stimulating problems relating to the laws governing natural phenomena. Thus, for those allied with the advance of natural philosophy there was hardly any need for ontological speculation. Nevertheless metaphysics was not completely abandoned, as we have seen.

For the sake of historical breadth it would be wise to briefly examine the works of some of the philosophers after Hume in order to find out if the course he indicated actually was followed. One of Hume's contemporaries, Lord James Burnett Monboddo, proposed a return to the "ancient science of universals" as a "philosophical" answer to Hume. He complains of the "wild and extravagant notions" which have "brought so great a disgrace upon the noblest of all sciences." [3] He refers to metaphysics, which he identifies with theology, or first philosophy, as a doctrine of mind separated from all body. Monboddo's views are not unusual, and his remarks evidence the disrepute of metaphysics in the latter half of the eighteenth century. He attributes this decline in part to the Newtonians but chiefly to Hume. Another critic of Hume, Thomas Reid, the founder of the so-called school of Scottish common-sense philosophy, remarks that sensible men, "who never will be skeptics in matters of common life, are apt to treat with sovereign contempt" everything that has been said on the subject of metaphysics. If sensible men find themselves "entangled in these metaphysical coils" Reid recommends

[3] Lord James Burnett Monboddo, *Ancient Metaphysics or the Science Universals* (Edinburgh, 1779), Introduction, p. 5.

that they cut the knot and curse metaphysics. But he adds:

> Is it absolutely certain that this fair lady [metaphysics] is of the party? Is it not possible she may have been [mis]represented? Have not men of genius in former ages often made their own dreams to pass for her oracles? Ought she then to be condemned without any further hearing? This would be unreasonable. I have found her in all other matters an agreeable companion, a faithful counsellor, a friend to common sense, and to the happiness of mankind.[4]

The matter in which metaphysics betrays the sensible man is the existence of the self, of other things and reliability of human reason. It is Hume, the skeptic, that Reid denounces and blames for the bad reputation of metaphysics, but he is careful to defend the name of traditional metaphysics and separate it from the metaphysical arguments of Hume to which he objects.

Reid and Monboddo are examples of the conservative reaction to Hume, and not surprisingly, they recommend a return to more traditional kinds of metaphysics. However, if we advance a generation or so we find a more interesting conception of metaphysics that reflects the acceptance of Hume's position. Dugald Stewart was a student and disciple of Reid and, like Reid and Monboddo, he begins his discussion of metaphysics by remarking about the great prejudice against it. After admitting that this prejudice is justified to a large extent, he singles out certain subjects of metaphysics which he thinks are of importance to "the useful arts and sciences" and for which there is a better "degree of evidence."[5] He has in mind the study of the phenomena of the human mind, and

---

[4] Thomas Reid, *The Philosophy of Reid as Contained in the Inquiry into the Human Mind*, with introduction and notes by E. H. Sneath (New York: H. Holt & Co., 1892), 87–88.

[5] Dugald Stewart, *Elements of the Philosophy of the Human Mind*, 5th ed., 3 vols. (London, 1814), 1 : 5.

he uses the term "phenomena" in order to repudiate any concern with the real nature or essence of the mind. He points out that physical science has been successful because it has put aside all problems concerning the real nature of matter, and even of its reality, and confined itself to "the humbler province of observing the phenomena it exhibits." [6] Stewart proposes a similar program for the study of the human mind, dismissing all questions relating to its real nature and confining himself to the study of its effects, which he considers to be as "factual" as the effects of matter that are studied in physics.

Stewart's proposition confirms our general remarks concerning the emergence of an independent science of the human mind or understanding. This science is to be free of ontological considerations, as Stewart makes unequivocally clear. Using a technique that should be quite familiar by now, he selects a subject from that receptacle of discredited knowledge called "metaphysics" and exalts it as legitimate and useful. The remaining contents of this receptacle, subjects concerning the real nature of mind or matter (ontology), are to be ignored and may retain the pejorative epithet of "metaphysics." Stewart's science or philosophy of the human mind is what Hume called "true metaphysics," but considering the disrepute of metaphysics, Stewart tries to dissociate his subject from it. However, the lengthy defensive introduction to his work indicates that he was aware of laying himself open to the charge of being a metaphysician. Hume also wrote a lengthy defensive introduction to the *Enquiry*, in which he tried to separate his own work, the true metaphysics, from the "fruitless efforts of human vanity," which "would penetrate into subjects utterly inaccessible to the understanding." [7] His opponents did not hesitate to call his work bad metaphysics, while those following in the direction he indicated sought to disassociate

[6] *Ibid.*
[7] Hume, *Enquiry*, Introduction, p. 11.

the study of the understanding from metaphysics. By Stewart's time, at the end of the eighteenth century, the study of human understanding was well on its way to being recognized as a subject separate from metaphysics.

Another interesting reference to metaphysics in Stewart's work, from a different point of view, provides us with a rather neat conclusion to our study. In discussing the term "cause," Stewart distinguishes two meanings. In the first place,

> when it is said that every change in nature indicates the operation of a cause, the word *cause* expresses something which is supposed to be necessarily connected with the change; and without which it could not have happened. This may be called the *metaphysical* meaning of the word; and such causes may be called metaphysical or efficient causes.[8]

Secondly, in natural philosophy "causes" refer to things or changes that are "constantly conjoined; so that when we see the one, we may expect the other." These are "*physical* causes." The influence of Hume is evident. Stewart accepts his interpretation of cause, crediting him with demonstrating that we have no right to assume a necessary connection between cause and effect. Stewart speaks of physical causes with approval, for this is the kind of cause dealt with in natural philosophy and also the kind of cause he recommends as proper for his philosophy of mind. He disapproves of metaphysical, or efficient, causes since they are supposed to go beyond sense data, or "phenomena." The interesting thing is that he identifies metaphysical cause and efficient cause. If we recall Bacon's conception of metaphysics as the study of formal (and final) causes and also Hobbes's treatment of formal causes as opposed to efficient causes it becomes clear that the notion of cause has taken a full turn during these two centuries. Bacon relegated efficient causes to physics and rated them as

[8] Stewart, *Elements of the Philosophy of the Human Mind*, 1:72.

somewhat inferior or deficient when compared with the formal causes of metaphysics. Hobbes rejected formal cause as a spurious notion and maintained that only material and efficient causes were meaningful. The notion of efficient cause with its model of bodies in motion striking one another was a central conception in his materialistic ontology. Thus, at mid-seventeenth century the notion of efficient cause was philosophically respectable, to say the least. But by the end of the eighteenth century Stewart considered "efficient cause" synonymous with "metaphysical cause." Neither physics nor the philosophy of mind was supposed to have anything to do with efficient cause; the notion of things or changes constantly conjoined had replaced it. Metaphysics, once supposed to be the study of formal causes, came to be known as the study of efficient causes. Stewart's conception of metaphysics is almost a complete reversal of Bacon's and the "true metaphysics," the science of human understanding, that Hume proposed seemed to be well started at the beginning of the nineteenth century with the work of Stewart. Generally speaking, during this period of two centuries the science of ultimate reality turned into a kind of phenomenological psychology.

Bibliography

Primary Sources

Algarotti, Francesco. *Sir Isaac Newton's Theory of Light and Colors.* Translated from the original Italian. 2 vols. London, 1742.

Aristotle. *The Basic Works of Aristotle.* Edited, with an introduction, by Richard McKeon. New York: Random House, 1941.

Bacon, Francis. *The Philosophical Works of Francis Bacon.* Edited, with an introduction, by John M. Robertson. London: George Routledge & Sons, 1905.

Barrow, Isaac. *Mathematical Lectures.* London, 1734.

Berkeley, George. *De Motu. Works,* vol. 4. Edited by A. A. Luce and T. E. Jessop. New York: T. Nelson, 1964.

———. *An Essay towards a New Theory of Vision. Works,* vol. 1. Edited by A. A. Luce and T. E. Jessop. New York: T. Nelson, 1964.

———. *Three Dialogues between Hylas and Philonous. Works,* vol. 2. Edited by A. A. Luce and T. E. Jessop. New York: T. Nelson, 1964.

———. *Treatise concerning the Principles of Human Knowledge. Works,* vol. 2. Edited by A. A. Luce and T. E. Jessop. New York: T. Nelson, 1964.

Cheyne, George. *Philosophical Principles of Religion, Natural and Revealed.* London: George Strahan, 1734.

Clarke, Samuel. *A Collection of Papers which Passed between the Late Learned Mr. Leibniz and Dr. Clarke in the Years 1715 and 1716 Relating to the Principles of Natural Philosophy and Religion.* London, 1717.

Cudworth, Ralph. *The True Intellectual System of the Universe.* Translated by J. Harrison. 3 vols. London, 1845.

Descartes, René. *The Principles of Philosophy.* In *The Philosophical Works of Descartes.* Translated by Elizabeth S. Haldane and G. R. T. Ross. 2 vols. Cambridge: Cambridge University Press, 1911.

Hobbes, Thomas. *The English Works of Thomas Hobbes.* Collected and edited by Sir William Molesworth. 16 vols. London: John Bohn, 1839–40.

————. *Leviathan.* 1651. With an essay by W. G. Pogson Smith. Oxford: Clarendon Press, 1909.

Hume, David. *An Enquiry concerning Human Understanding*, in *Hume's Enquiries* 2nd edition by L. A. Selby-Bigge (Oxford: Clarendon Press, 1966). Reprinted from the posthumous edition of 1777.

————. *A Treatise of Human Nature.* 3 vols. Edited by L. A. Selby-Bigge. Oxford: Clarendon Press, 1888.

Keill, John. *An Introduction to Natural Philosophy.* 4th ed. London, 1745.

Locke, John. *An Essay concerning Human Understanding.* Collated and annotated, with prolegomena, by Alexander Campbell Fraser. 2 vols. New York: Dover Publications, 1959.

Monboddo, Lord James Burnett. *Ancient Metaphysics or the Science of Universals.* Edinburgh, 1779.

More, Henry. *An Antidote against Atheism.* In *A Collection of Several Philosophical Writings.* 4th ed. London: Joseph Downing, 1711.

Newton, Isaac. *Mathematical Principles of Natural Philosophy.* Translated by Andrew Motte in 1729. Revised by Florian Cajori. Berkeley: University of California Press, 1934.

————. *Optics.* In *Newton's Philosophy of Nature.* Edited by H. S. Thayer. New York: Hafner Publishing Co., Hafner Library of Classics, 1953.

Ockham, William of. *Quodlibeta.* In *Selections from Medieval Philosophers.* Edited and translated, with introductory notes and glossary, by Richard McKeon. Vol. 2. New York: Charles Scribner's Sons, 1930.

Reid, Thomas. *The Philosophy of Reid as Contained in the Inquiry into the Human Mind.* Introduction and notes by E. H. Sneath. New York: H. Holt and Co., 1892.

Sargeant, John. *Solid Philosophy Asserted against the Fancies of the Ideists.* London, 1697.

Shaftesbury, Anthony Ashley Cooper, third Earl of. *Characteristics of Men, Manners, Opinions, Times.* 3 vols. Birmingham, 1773.

Sprat, Thomas. *History of the Royal Society of London.* London, 1667.

Stewart, Dugald. *Elements of the Philosophy of the Human Mind.* 5th ed. 3 vols. London, 1814.

Secondary Sources

Anderson, Robert Fendel. *Hume's First Principles.* Lincoln: University of Nebraska Press, 1965.

Boas, Marie. "The Establishment of the Mechanical Philosophy." *Osiris, Commentationes de Scientiarum et Eruditionis Historia Rationeque.* Edited by Georgius Sarton. Vol. 10. Brugis: Ex Officina "De Tempel," 1952.

Brett, George S. *Brett's History of Psychology.* Edited by R. S. Peters. New York: Macmillan Co., 1953.

Burtt, Edwin Arthur. *The Metaphysical Foundations of Modern Physical Science.* Rev. ed. Garden City, N.Y.: Doubleday & Co., 1954.

Doney, Willis. "Nicolas Malebranche." In *The Encyclopedia of Philosophy.* Vol. 5. New York: Macmillan Co. and the Free Press, 1967.

Forsyth, Thomas M. *English Philosophy.* London: Adam and Charles Black, 1910.

Fuller, B. A. G. *A History of Philosophy.* Rev. ed. New York: Henry Holt & Co., 1945.

Hurlbutt, Robert H. III. *Hume, Newton, and the Design Argument.* Lincoln: University of Nebraska Press, 1965.

Laird, John. *Hobbes.* London: Ernest Benn, 1934.

Lowrey, Charles E. *The Philosophy of Ralph Cudworth.* New York: Phillips & Hunt, 1884.

Luce, A. A. *Berkeley and Malebranche.* London: Humphrey Milford, 1934.

————. *The Life of George Berkeley.* New York: Thomas Nelson & Sons, 1949.

Mackinnon, Flora Isabel. *Philosophical Writings of Henry More.* New York: Oxford University Press, 1925.

Mayo, Thomas Franklin. *Epicurus in England (1650–1725).* Dallas: Southwest Press, 1934.

Morris, George S. *British Thought and Thinkers.* Chicago: S. C. Griggs & Co., 1880.

Passmore, John. *Hume's Intentions.* New York: Basic Books, Inc., 1968.

Pepper, S. C. *World Hypotheses: A Study in Evidence.* Berkeley: University of California Press, 1948.

Pepper, Steven C. Karl Aschenbrenner, Benson Mates, et al. *George Berkeley.* University of California Publications in Philosophy, vol. 29. Berkeley: University of California Press, 1957.

Price, H. H. *Thinking and Experience.* London: Hutchinson's University Library, 1953.

Robertson, G. C. *Hobbes.* Edinburgh: Wm. Blackwood & Sons, 1886.

Seth, James. *English Philosophers and Schools of Philosophy.* London: J. M. Dent & Sons, 1912.

Smith, Norman Kemp. *The Philosophy of David Hume.* New York: Macmillan, 1960.

Stephen, Leslie. *History of English Thought in the Eighteenth Century.* 2 vols., 3d ed. London: Smith, Elder & Co., 1902.

———. *Hobbes.* London: Macmillan & Co., 1928.

Strong, Edward W. "Newton and God." *Journal of the History of Ideas* 13 (1952): 147–67.

———. "Newtonian Explications of Natural Philosophy." *Journal of the History of Ideas* 17 (1957): 49–83.

Taylor, A. E. *Thomas Hobbes.* London: Archibald Constable & Co., 1908.

Turbayne, Colin M. Introduction to *Three Dialogues* by George Berkeley. New York: Liberal Arts Press, 1954.

Weber, Alfred. *History of Philosophy.* Translated by Frank Thilly. New York: Charles Scribner's Sons, 1925.

Wild, John. *George Berkeley.* New York: Russell & Russell, Inc., 1962.

Willey, Basil. *The Seventeenth Century Background.* Garden City, N.Y.: Doubleday & Co., Doubleday Anchor Books, 1953.

Windelband, Wilhelm. *A History of Philosophy.* Authorized translation by James H. Tufts. 2d ed. New York: Macmillan Co., 1901.

Yolton, John W. *John Locke and the Way of Ideas.* London: Oxford University Press, 1956.

Zabeeh, Farhang. *Hume, Precursor of Modern Empiricism.* The Hague: Martinus Nijhoff, 1960.

Acknowledgments

I AM INDEBTED to my teachers Edward W. Strong, Celestine J. Sullivan, William R. Dennes, Stephen C. Pepper, Colin M. Turbayne, Benson Mates and Robert H. Hurlbutt. Professor Strong has been especially helpful in providing both criticism and encouragement in equal measure. I owe as well a special gratitude to my good friends and fellow philosophers, Erik Bauersfeld, Bill Charles, and Tosun Suvor.

Index